Beyond the Myth of Self-Esteem

Finding Fulfilment

John Smith
with Coral Chamberlain

ACORN PRESS

Published by Acorn Press Ltd
ABN 50 008 549 540

Office and orders:
PO Box 258
Moreland VIC 3058
Australia
Tel/Fax: (03) 9383 1266
International Tel/Fax: 61 3 9383 1266
Website: www.acornpress.net.au

© Kevin John Smith 2014

National Library of Australia Cataloguing-in-Publication entry:

Creator:	Smith, Kevin John, 1942– author.
Title:	Beyond the myth of self-esteem: finding fulfilment/ John Smith with Coral Chamberlain.
ISBN:	9780992447632 (paperback)
	9780992447649 (ebook)
Subjects:	Self-esteem.
	Self.
	Identity (Psychology)
	Faith.
Other Authors/Contributors:	Chamberlain, Coral.
Dewey Number:	158.1

Apart from any fair dealing for the purposes of private study, research, criticism or review, no part of this work may be reproduced by electronic or other means without the permission of the publisher.

WHEN YOU WISH UPON A STAR. Words by Ned Washington Music by Leigh Harline. © Copyright 1940 by Bourne Co. Copyright Renewed. All Rights Reserved International Copyright Secured. ASCAP.

Unless otherwise indicated, Bible quotations are from *THE HOLY BIBLE, NEW INTERNATIONAL VERSION®, NIV®* Copyright © 1973, 1978, 1984, 2011 by Biblica, Inc.® Used by permission. All rights reserved worldwide.

One Bible quotation is from *The Message*. Copyright © 1993, 1994, 1995, 1996, 2000, 2001, 2002. Used by permission of NavPress Publishing Group.

Editors: Gina Denholm & Kristin Argall.
Cover design: Antony Brown.
Text design and layout: Gretchen Berquist Gordon.
Printed by: Openbook Howden Design & Print.

To my wife Glena and my family for their loving support, and for keeping me on track through often difficult times

Contents

	Preface	vii
1.	Self-Esteem, Self-Respect or Self-Obsession?	1
2.	The Be-Whatever-You-Want-To-Be Myth	8
3.	The You-Must-Feel-Good-Look-Good Myth	16
4.	The Boosting-Self-Esteem-Brings-Happiness Myth	28
5.	The All-About-Me Myth	44
6.	The Never-My-Fault Myth	63
7.	Gurus of the Myth of Self-Esteem	74
8.	A Rising Tide of Dissent	94
9.	How Have We Become So Self-Oriented?	112
10.	The Impact of Self-Esteem Myths on Society	127
11.	Finding Identity and Meaning	141
12.	Exploring the Spiritual Dimension	156
13.	The Most Seductive Myth of All	166
14.	Self-Esteem and Self-Surrender: The Ultimate Paradox	178
	Acknowledgements	187
	Notes	191

Preface

I have lived most of my life in suburban middle-class comfort, and I share many of the privileges and aspirations of the average citizen in the Western world. However, I have been experiencing a growing unease. Pleasant evenings chatting with people in pubs, adrenalin-charged hours on a motorcycle with outlaw acquaintances, and disturbing experiences with homeless young people, broken families and the working poor have tempered my confidence in our current system, with its emphasis on the pursuit of success and individual happiness.

My involvement, since the late 1960s, in lifestyle seminar presentations in many thousands of secondary schools has helped me keep in touch with the monumental changes in beliefs, institutions, popular culture and family structures that have taken place over the years. We live in exciting and exhilarating times, it is true. We marvel at human potential and the wide range of options that are now available to the individual. For many of us, life seems good and happiness achievable – and yet, I am concerned about what I am seeing.

It was in part this concern that drove me to move to the USA in the mid-1990s to pursue six years of research and doctoral studies. I was seeking to understand the impact, causes and significance of vast changes I saw occurring as we approached the twenty-first century. Like David Suzuki, David Attenborough and others who share their views, I am passionate about the survival of the planet in all its glorious diversity. As a father, and a survivor–thriver of a long partnership with a warm and vibrant wife and mother, I care deeply about my children and my grandchildren. I also care about yours, and the future they will inherit.

I feel that we need to discover a sense of being part of a healthy community, of being individuals united in a commitment that goes beyond the distraction of self-obsession. Interestingly, the ideas presented in this book may perhaps be more pertinent now in the context of global economic and climatic crisis than would have been apparent just a few years ago, when greed was good and enlightened self-interest was the driver for a more prosperous and fulfilling life.

I bring to this book an experience of the joy of being fully alive to something much bigger than myself. I now realise that the search for a sense of accomplishment, fulfilment and belonging is quite distinct from the current fascination with the isolated self. One of the world's most influential visionaries long ago asserted that to find ourselves we must lose ourselves to a greater vision. He also said that discovering this truth is liberating.

I am inviting you to come on a journey with me to explore a new way of living, a way of living that liberates us from the confines of an obsession with self and self-esteem. But be warned. This book will challenge almost all you have ever heard or read about self-esteem as expressed by contemporary popular culture.

John Smith

1

Self-Esteem, Self-Respect or Self-Obsession?

In Western cultures, there are many different views about what will make us happy. Some see happiness in materialistic terms: if I have a good job and sufficient money to buy whatever I fancy, I will be happy. Others link happiness to human freedom: my financial situation may not be great but being able to do what I want to do, without censorship or regulation, is truly a happy existence. For some, relationships are the key to happiness: if I have a good relationship with my partner, my children and my work colleagues, then I will be happy. Others seek happiness by detachment from relational demands or limitations.

Of course, the very definition of happiness is open to debate. A millionaire may appear to be happy but show less serenity and wisdom than a homeless person.

Social commentator Clive Hamilton describes three ways of viewing happiness or wellbeing: *the pleasant life, the good life* and *the meaningful life*.[1] *The pleasant life*, he says, is a life that produces a sense of pleasure. It is about maximising emotional and physical highs, and it centres on achieving financial independence, as this gives people the capacity to build a pleasureable lifestyle. *The good life* is about fulfilling personal potential, pursuing dreams and developing innate capacities. Again, the focus is still very clearly on the self. *The meaningful life* goes beyond these, to a life committed to something larger than self – a higher cause of some kind.

Some of us would say that happiness comes from knowing that our life has meaning and purpose. Even through tough times, we can have a sense of dignity and significance that brings peace and fulfilment. In this context, self-respect may seem of greater importance than self-esteem. Social researcher Hugh Mackay expresses this view when he writes:

> Overly hyped self-esteem can slip very easily into vanity, arrogance and triumphalism, whereas self-respect is our personal, private reward for living in ways that are true to our noblest and loftiest ideals – especially those concerned with the wellbeing of others.[2]

Self-esteem has become an almost ubiquitous term. It permeates pop-culture journalism and the books on the shelves in the self-help, business and spirituality sections of commercial outlets, creating a bonanza for motivational speakers, TV gurus and pop psychologists.[3] It is now such common currency that it is mentioned in almost any discussion of youth affairs, gender conflict, education and even popular religion.

Thirty years ago, self-esteem barely rated a mention in the popular press.[4] Now a Google search for this term yields more than 30 million hits. Many factors have contributed to this explosion of interest in self-esteem, as later chapters will reveal. Here, I want simply to draw attention to a few of the key events that have brought us to this point.[5]

The first purely psychological use of the term self-esteem can be traced back to 1890 and the work of William James, who is often referred to as the father of modern psychology. However, self-esteem did not even begin to emerge as an influential idea among psychologists and academics until the late 1960s, when, with the rise of wealth and consumerism, it became easier to conceptualise the individual at the centre of his or her destiny.

A significant figure in the emerging focus on self-esteem was psychotherapist Nathaniel Branden.[6] He was a devotee of philosopher Ayn Rand, who through her novels was a strong proponent of radical individualism and enlightened self-interest. Branden is regarded as the intellectual father of what is now called 'the self-esteem movement', which extended his ideas into popular culture. It must be said, however, that many popular beliefs about self-esteem and the strategies advocated for boosting self-esteem are a far cry from both his original concepts and those he now espouses. It is as though he opened the stable door for a horse that has since bolted out of his control.

It was not until the late 1980s that the concept of self-esteem moved out of academia and the clinic and into public awareness. This was largely because of its perceived political implications. John Vasconcellos, a member of the California State Assembly, proposed that low self-esteem was the cause of crime, teenage pregnancy, drug abuse and school underachievement. He became an influential and successful advocate of a policy aimed at boosting young people's self-esteem as a 'social vaccine'.

Vasconcellos also argued that boosting self-esteem would help balance the state budget, because those with high self-esteem would earn more money and so pay more tax. A task force set up as a result of his efforts continued operating until 1990. It was then replaced by the still-active National Association for Self-Esteem (NASE), committed to fully integrating self-esteem into the fabric of American society – within families, schools, the government and the workplace.

Despite a lack of evidence for Vasconcellos' initial claims, and the discouraging results of numerous studies since then, the idea that boosting self-esteem can vaccinate against all kinds of societal ills, personal failures and inner problems persisted. Rather than fading with time, this faddish notion flourished and became incorporated into the emerging self-esteem movement.

Unlike most fads, the general fascination with self-esteem did not simply run its course and disappear. Instead, throughout the Western world, attractive but unsubstantiated beliefs about self-esteem gradually became woven into the fabric of popular culture. As a result, over time, the teachings of the self-esteem movement were transformed into a powerful cultural myth, that is, a collective belief built up in response to people's wishes rather than a rational analysis of the situation.[7] I call this *the myth of self-esteem*. This overarching myth encompasses many individual myths. Anyone born since the 1980s in the Western world is likely to have lived their entire life under the influence of myths about self-esteem, at least to some extent.

I have taken a keen interest in the emergence of this phenomenon and its impact on the individual and society for many years. As I have delved and discussed, listened and pondered, I have come to recognise the following as characteristics of the myth of self-esteem:

- isolation of the individual from traditional social relationships
- an assumption that life is a level playing field, that anyone can succeed in finding the 'pleasant life' and the 'good life'
- an emphasis on feeling good and looking good
- an emphasis on trusting and acting on feelings in relation to heart aspirations
- a prioritisation of personal success over social responsibility
- a justification of self-focus by the assertion that we must love ourselves before we can love others
- a spirituality defined by personal fulfilment rather than divine or cultural expectations.

In subsequent chapters, I will return to each of these points, highlight individual self-esteem myths associated with them and provide

Self-Esteem, Self-Respect or Self-Obsession?

my rationale for including them.[8] My thinking has been shaped not only by academic delving but also by powerful life experiences and by my close connections with people in many strata of society – in my home country, Australia, and throughout the world.

Because the teachings of the myth of self-esteem have become so deeply embedded in Western culture, they are virtually unrecognisable as myth. I therefore devote a large part of this book to bringing these teachings and their consequences to light, so you, the reader, are in a position to make your own evaluation. Chapters 2–6 identify and describe individual myths that are part of the myth of self-esteem and explain some of their pitfalls. Chapter 7 describes 'gurus' of the myth of self-esteem: influential people who, whether they are aware of it or not, have effectively promulgated the teachings of the myth over the years. Chapters 8–10 look at factors I believe have made us, as individuals and societies, particularly vulnerable to assimilating the teachings of the myth and experiencing the global consequences of that process.

The final four chapters, Chapters 11–14, turn to the quest for identity and meaning, and the role of the spiritual dimension of life in bringing true fulfilment and deep joy. These are the chapters I have most enjoyed writing. I can well imagine that you may be tempted to hop and skip your way through earlier chapters to get to these key chapters quickly. You may do that, of course, but I suspect you will find that reading this book is a bit like reading a mystery novel. You will get more out of it if you follow the 'plot' as it unfolds than you will if you skip to the last few pages to find out how it ends.

The ancient Greek myth about *Narcissus* seems to be finding new relevance in the postmodern cultures of today's affluent societies.

> *Narcissus, cursed by the gods to be infatuated with the first human face he saw, happened upon a deep pool of water. Seeing his own face reflected in its smooth surface, he fell instantly in love with his own image. When he*

> touched the surface of the water, to his dismay, the image became distorted. Such was his fanatical obsession with his image that he could not bear to lose sight of it for a moment. He could not disturb the pool in order to drink or move from it to obtain food. Pathetically, he sat there and wasted away.

Over the last few decades, many psychologists and social analysts have spoken of our modern and postmodern societies as being, in broad terms, profoundly narcissistic.[9] We are in danger of becoming so obsessed with self-image and self-esteem that our lives are diverted from productive paths onto the bypath of a self-obsession that borders on destructive self-worship.

The nurturing of self-esteem, now widely perceived to be an important means of achieving success, seems to have become an end in itself.[10] Low self-esteem tends to be regarded as a primary problem, which must be addressed directly by a whole array of self-esteem-boosting techniques, rather than as one of the results or symptoms of a more profound personal dysfunction or a failure of modern and postmodern culture.

The self-esteem-boosting strategies presented to us, often as part of a slick and expensive self-improvement package, seem so much more attractive and doable than addressing underlying personal, spiritual and societal issues. Yet, it may be much more important to deal with the latter if we are to achieve happy, satisfying and meaningful lives.

I am not suggesting that all the insights to be found in presentations and books that extol the importance of self-esteem are unhelpful. Nor am I saying that we should have a negative view of ourselves or life – quite the contrary. However, I am convinced that there are destructive flaws in the confident communications of unregulated, market-driven, self-proclaimed 'experts' in this field. I am concerned about the widespread and growing acceptance of a culture of pleasure and self-gratification that amounts, in some cases, to a compulsion to feel good about oneself at all times and an excessive need for enjoyable experiences.

This culture is promoted by many who wield great influence in society. Their assertions, if presented with sufficient charisma on the right TV channels or at a motivational seminar in the presence of an applauding audience, have a huge impact on individuals exposed to them. They also generate substantial incomes for the presenters, with the possibility of bestseller listing in *The New York Times*. If their theories are flawed, then we have among us many people who are the products of a well-intentioned but misguided crusade – one that has the potential to leave in its wake an epidemic of disillusionment and despair.

In days gone by, when gold was discovered, the news spread rapidly and people rushed to the site. Sometimes it was a false alarm or the supply was small. For all those who returned gloriously enriched, there were just as many who went home having spent all they had for nothing. A key question in relation to self-esteem is this: how much is real gold and how much is fool's gold? My purpose is not to deny the existence of some gold. It is to question some dangerous exaggerations and mistaken views about the significance of self-esteem as the source, rather than the result, of a truly successful, meaningful life.

My clear message is this: *there is more to life than the nurturing of our self-esteem*. Many people are already abandoning that pursuit in favour of the search for meaning and fulfilment. My hope is that this book will open many more hearts and minds to the possibility of a new and more satisfying way of living.

2

The Be-Whatever-You-Want-To-Be Myth

When you wish upon a star
Makes no difference who you are
Anything your heart desires
Will come to you.[1]

An explicit assumption of the myth of self-esteem is that, no matter who you are, you can be whatever you want to be. Through common usage, this assertion has become a motivational catchphrase, almost a mantra, which few seem to challenge. Backing this up is the increasing illusion that life is getting better for all who really want it to happen.

Is the sky the limit?

There is a whole genre of movies that portray an exceptional individual who succeeds against enormous odds – *Invictus*, *Schindler's List* and *Defiance* are some examples. Such movies can be inspirational, encouraging our spirit and motivating us. They can also be unhelpful if we take the rare instance and turn it into a personal maxim for life: I too can achieve greatness, I too can be whatever I want to be.

We need to remember that the inspiring individuals who are the focus of these movies defy the normal principle. Nelson Mandela, for example, achieved great and worthy goals, but most black Africans of that time had no way of rising out of obscurity. While marvelling at Schindler's efforts in rescuing more than a thousand Jewish people from the Holocaust, we can similarly forget that millions of wonderful people died excruciating deaths.

In 2010 Jessica Watson, a 16-year-old yachtswoman, completed a solo around-the-world voyage for which she was later named Young Australian of the Year. When she eventually disembarked in Sydney, she told the huge crowd waiting to greet her, 'I'm an ordinary girl who believed in a dream. You just have to have a dream, believe in it and work hard.'

I applaud wholeheartedly Jessica's stamina and courage, but I disagree that she is just an ordinary girl. First, Jessica is genetically and emotionally equipped to exhibit physical abilities, endurance and determination far beyond the norm for her age. Second, she lived for years on a boat with her parents, was thoroughly tutored in the seagoing craft from primary school age and was later trained specifically by experts in the field. Third, she received extraordinary financial backing, which provided a suitable yacht, equipped with costly high-tech navigation and communications systems, as well as consistent support for her along the way.

There appears to be insufficient recognition that our lives are affected by many forces that are beyond our control, either individually or as a society. There is still much debate about whether nature (our genetics) or nurture (family and social conditioning) has the greater influence on our development as individuals. Current evidence, as I understand it, is this: while our genetic makeup – our unique biological inheritance – does impose limits on what we can be, our physical attributes and our future are not inevitably determined by our genes. Other factors such as our environment, our social grouping's views, our education and our personal experiences, provide us with the possibility of a wide variety of outcomes.

To this extent it is true that we can each exercise choice to make the best of our capabilities. If we are sufficiently motivated, we can become the best possible version of ourselves, given the limits of our personal, physical, social, environmental, and political reality. But to say that we can be whatever we want to be is self-evident nonsense. The possibilities open to us will be circumscribed by our inherent physical and personal attributes, our intellectual capacity, the presence or absence of disability or chronic – even terminal – illness, our financial and social status, and the culture or country in which we live. Even the enormously wealthy and brilliant founder of the Apple corporation, Steve Jobs, was not able to be whatever he wanted to be. He died of cancer aged 56, at the peak of his abilities.

Leaping the bar

According to Clive Hamilton,

> For large majorities of the citizens of wealthy democratic countries there are no significant external obstacles to fulfilling their capabilities. For them the question is no longer whether they are *able* to flourish, but whether they will choose to do so.[2]

At first glance, Hamilton's comments may appear to be endorsing the be-whatever-you-want-to be myth, but this is not his intention. He is talking about a specific, privileged subset of the global population – those in 'wealthy democratic countries' – not all people. He is talking about *external obstacles*, as distinct from inherent and acquired characteristics that cannot be changed; about fulfilling our *capabilities*, not our wildest dreams.

It can be argued that motivational seminars, classes, literature and movies that promote the be-whatever-you-want-to-be myth may be helpful to a small minority of already highly motivated, genetically blessed and culturally well-positioned individuals. But for the vast majority of people, such presentations are simply reinforcing a myth of the impossible. The high jump bar of expectations is raised beyond the attainable. Only the few who are suitably endowed leap over the bar and soar to the excellence presented and promised. If you believe the myth and are one of the many who do not make it over the bar, you have to suffer not only the associated disappointment but also the sense of guilt and failure arising from your poor performance.

To maintain the myth, negative outcomes can always be attributed to a failure to 'listen to your authentic self' or 'follow your heart' – in pop psychology terms – or to insufficient effort, motivation or acquired skills on your part to achieve your goal. Accordingly, those who do achieve are to be admired for fulfilling their destiny and diligently investing their potentiality. Those who do not are relegated to the position of second-class losers who have failed to use their natural human endowments.

This attitude overlooks the influences that are independent of the individual's giftedness and sincere effort – things such as social advantage and connections, changes in political and economic conditions and genetic inheritance. Such factors predispose many who are in the 'loser' category to retreat after a few genuine attempts to be whatever it is they want to be. It is not only those who are less talented who suffer. Those who cannot find employment following redundancy must either live in denial or face the fact that they cannot be what they want to be. The creative but non-conformist fringe, who do not aspire to the norms that are supposedly indicative of success and healthy self-esteem, may also find themselves written off.

I feel for children who are not naturally courageous and never will be. I feel for young people who, in the terms of success as defined by our culture, are not particularly capable or naturally endowed. Their humanness is of unquestionable value. If, however, their eyes are fixed unrealistically on high achievement or an academic career, this is unlikely to be a self-esteem-boosting exercise. It is more likely that they will suffer disillusionment and dejection – in some cases, even serious depression. What is more, at this early stage of their lives, their failure to achieve may become a serious deterrent to their quest for self-improvement.

One factor fostering acceptance of this particular myth may be that it tells us what we want to hear. It feels good to think that anyone can achieve what they want, as long as they are prepared to believe the mantra and put in the effort. The unpalatable alternative is to face the reality of the social disadvantage and poverty that exists side by side with wealth and self-indulgence in our society.

It is not hard to understand why the be-whatever-you-want-to-be myth has gained such acceptance in prosperous Western societies. But for people living in developing countries, where many suffer oppression and structural poverty, it makes little sense. Few in this situation have much hope of achieving even their most modest dreams.

Logic should tell us it is impossible for all to achieve their dreams under these conditions. Nevertheless, I am aware that, in Africa, the desperate desire of the poor to escape from poverty and powerlessness, combined with access to global TV, is enticing many to believe this widely presented myth. It is clearly a misleading assessment of their reality: the more likely outcome is that a growing minority of people in countries like Africa, India and Asia will join the global millionaires' club, leaving the majority poor behind.

An unlevel playing field

Those of us who have a role in serving the poor and marginalised are painfully aware that, even in affluent countries, sub-groups are still trapped in circumstances of extreme disadvantage and misery, their situations offering little if any hope of fulfilling their dreams. Discrimination based on financial and social status, ethnicity and religion abounds. The you-can-be-whatever-you-want-to-be catchphrase has a decidedly hollow ring when applied to those on the margins who struggle daily to meet the costs of basic necessities.

The Be-Whatever-You-Want-To-Be Myth

Here is just one of many stories I could tell:

> *In New Orleans during Mardi Gras, my wife Glena and I wandered the streets at night. As we walked back to our motel on the outskirts of town in the early morning, we met a pleasant 'bag lady'. Beside her was a shopping trolley containing all her worldly possessions. A storm hit, with torrential rain. Outside a nearby bank stood a guard who was intent on denying her shelter under the awning of an adjacent shop – a small luxury forbidden by council regulation. She would have to sleep on the edge of the kerb in the pouring rain under a sheet of plastic. We returned shortly to bring her some food, and the reassurance of human care and touch. She was a gentle middle-aged woman of positive faith, but without either employment or prospects. She usually slept on a park bench and showered at the local hospital. In the face of our obvious horror at her situation, she was quite positive about a lifestyle she had come to accept.*

On hearing such stories, some may automatically blame the individual for failing to make a success of their lives. However, the reality of the issue is much more complex. For example, we now know that many who live in extreme poverty do so mainly because of mental health problems. I have great sympathy for those who suffer mental disorders that put them at odds with the way society says a healthy mind should operate. Others are simply resigned to the fact that there is no foreseeable path to upward mobility open to them – physically, emotionally or socially.

Besides the extremity of the homeless street culture, there are other sub-groups whose circumstances severely limit their prospects of becoming whatever they want to be. These include the so-called working poor – those whose wages are insufficient to meet basic needs of housing, food, medicine and education – and people who must subsist on low welfare payments.

> *While residing in the Appalachian region of the USA during my years of graduate study, I met many people living in poverty. The appalling basic wage*

> was insufficient to meet minimal needs, even with both parents working.³ For a single-parent family and those on low welfare payments, conditions were often disastrous. Unexpected car problems could end a worker's employment if public transport was unavailable or unaffordable. An illness leading to loss of wages, or the breakdown of a refrigerator, could have catastrophic consequences. For many, decisions about the purchase of everyday items were an ongoing source of stress. Simple luxuries most of us would take for granted, like buying a cup of coffee, were out of the question.

American journalist and socio-economic analyst Gregg Easterbrook describes this new, deep structural problem in the West as 'money anguish'.[4] Few starve to death in the Western world, as they still do in massive numbers in the rest of the world, but people can nevertheless suffer from malnutrition, even while surrounded by supermarkets sporting twenty different choices of flour on the shelves and a vast array of pizza options.

The sad reality is that the option of participating in the be-whatever-you-want-to-be quest is a luxury available only to the most privileged in society, and it increasingly marks the gulf between the 'haves' and the 'have nots'.[5] What person living in poverty could afford the self-help books, courses, conferences and motivational DVDs that claim to assist people achieve their dreams? Even conferences of this genre organised by Christian groups and advertised on TV are far beyond the economic capacity of many who may wish they could attend. For the 'have nots', the inflated expectations fed by the be-whatever-you-want-to-be myth and related 'follow your dream' rhetoric may serve only to intensify their anguish.

In 2009 and beyond, as a result of the global financial crisis, we saw mass tragedies being played out, particularly in the American media, as people accustomed to a comfortable lifestyle were evicted from their homes because they were no longer able to meet their mortgage payments. At that time, in the USA and elsewhere, many in the generation that had been taught they could be anything they wanted to be suffered a painful reality check when they suddenly found themselves unemployed.

When you take a moment to think about it, it becomes obvious that, even in affluent societies, the level playing field with equal opportunities for all is an unsustainable myth. For the majority of people living in troubled, poverty-stricken nations, it seems no better than a cruel taunt.

Finding a sense of hope and working towards positive change, irrespective of our circumstances, is healthy. Living out the fantasy that every dream can be achieved is not.[6]

3

The You-Must-Feel-Good-Look-Good Myth

A pervasive tenet of the myth of self-esteem is that feeling good and looking good are not only expressions of high self-esteem but also important strategies for boosting and maintaining your self-esteem. The advertising world exploits this by providing us with a huge variety of 'feel good-look good' products and services, with catchcries such as *indulge yourself, pamper yourself, reward yourself (you deserve it)*, and *when you're comfortable, you can do anything*.[1] In such a world, an unhealthy preoccupation with feeling good and looking good becomes almost inevitable.

Feeling good

If we set aside the marginalised and disadvantaged people for whom life can be very difficult indeed, we have to acknowledge that life is good for most of us in Western societies. Gregg Easterbrook has listed the following as advantages achieved for the majority living in the USA at the beginning of the twenty-first century.[2] In general terms, these apply throughout the Western world:

- unlimited food at affordable prices and in enormous variety
- longer life expectancy – the average American lifespan has risen from 41 to 77 years over the last century[3]
- the defeat of history's plagues such as polio, smallpox, measles, and rickets, and a stunning reduction in infectious diseases thanks to antibiotics
- the end of backbreaking physical toil for most wage earners
- the arrival of leisure – the typical person now works, either for pay or within the household, for about half as many hours as in the nineteenth century
- the end of formal discrimination against minorities and women
- mass home ownership, with heated and cooled dwellings commonplace
- financial and medical care provided for growing numbers of senior citizens
- ready access to information, art and literature
- incredible advances in freedom – political freedom, freedom of expression, sexual freedom, freedom from military conscription.

Because life can indeed be good for many today, a perpetual state of feeling good may seem a natural and appropriate response. However, if we have a self-esteem-driven perception that we must at all times feel good – that experiencing unpleasant feelings, so-called 'negative feelings', is a hindrance to our quest for the good life – it is possible to deceive ourselves into feeling *good* in situations in which it would be more appropriate for us to be feeling *bad*.

I have found support for this personal belief in the comments of the eminent American academic and psychologist Martin Seligman. He says that in two generations, America and Australia have become feeling-good societies rather than doing-well societies. An element in the feeling-good self-esteem movement that he finds particularly concerning is the cushioning of dysphoria (i.e. anger, sadness and anxiety).[4]

Beyond the Myth of Self-Esteem

A few years ago I read a book by Paul Brand and Phillip Yancey, entitled *The Gift of Pain: Why We Hurt and What We Can Do about It*.[5] They were expressing their concern that our culture tends to see pain as something to be avoided at all cost. They did not propose that all pain is good or that we should go looking for it, but they provided compelling evidence that being able to feel pain is important.

Brand, a gifted orthopaedic surgeon, was the first to use reconstructive surgery to correct deformities in the hands and feet caused by leprosy, a disease that destroys the nerves. The appalling, disfiguring damage associated with this condition happens because sufferers lose the ability to feel and respond appropriately to pain. Because there is no pain to send a warning, severely damaged fingers and toes are not cared for and injuries become infected. Flesh is lost and the individual is maimed. In this situation, feeling good, instead of feeling bad, is a tragic lie.

Brand and Yancey provocatively take this notion even further. They describe our ability to feel physical, social and emotional pain as 'a gift from God' that provides us with the possibility of taking appropriate self-protective action. Their proposal reminds me of a man I met some years ago.

> *While travelling across Australia's vast Nullarbor Plain to Western Australia, Glena and I stopped at Kalgoorlie to visit the indigenous Ngaanyatjarra people, who had adopted me. There we met a one-legged man from the Maralinga region. His people had suffered terribly from the decision of the Australian Government to allow Britain to carry out atomic bomb testing on their tribal land during the 1950s and 1960s.[6] Now a broken people, they wander into white towns like Kalgoorlie and deaden their emotional pain with alcohol – to the profit of local white liquor establishments – until they intuitively sense they are close to the edge. They then wander back into the semi-arid scrub, only to repeat the pattern later.*
>
> *During our stay, this man chose to tell us his story. One night, out in the bush, he was so totally wiped out by alcohol that he rolled into the fire. The*

> desert can be very cold at night and fires must be lit – these people do not own high-tech sleeping bags. He was so drunk that he did not feel the pain as his leg was literally cooked. Fortunately, he survived amputation but he was still blotting out his physical and emotional pain with alcohol – his particular 'feel-good' drug.

Without pain, we would do unbelievable damage to ourselves. Hold a lit match between your fingers. To avoid intense pain, you will drop it instinctively before it damages your skin. Emotional pain can also serve a useful purpose. For example, if we treat our partner badly, it may be appropriate to experience the pain of being ostracised until we choose to improve our behaviour. Feeling the pain of failure can also work to our advantage. It can do even more for us than immediate success if we are prepared to question seriously why we failed. We can make use of the experience as an opportunity to grow in understanding of our circumstances or to change course and avoid failure next time.

Blotting out the pain

The society in which we live seduces us into seeking ways to blot out our bad feelings and create feel-good cocoons to protect ourselves from realities we do not want to accept. A huge variety of options are on offer to help us escape reality, some seemingly harmless, others obviously damaging. These include: a vast array of recreational and travel opportunities at prices many can afford, shop-till-you-drop 'retail therapy', readily available sex, caffeine-laced energy drinks, pain-killers and sedatives, alcohol, illegal mind-altering drugs, TV, music, computer gaming and social networking – even attending a feel-good motivational seminar. All can be used to anaesthetise us in one way or another, often against our best interests. Richard Rohr, a Franciscan priest and motivational speaker, believes that virtually all addictions are an attempt to find a palliative.[7] He suggests that it is a normal condition for people in contemporary society to be addicted in one way or another.

Workaholic behaviour is also a readily available palliative, made even more enticing by the prospect of making us feel good in the longer term through increased status and income.[8] Another feel-good manoeuvre is deluding ourselves and others into believing that we are competent in virtually every situation we encounter, quashing feelings of inferiority or embarrassment. Ironically, it is only when we own our lack of knowledge or experience that we open the door to gaining the very skills and qualities we would like to have.

My Aboriginal brother from the Maralinga region used alcohol as his feel-good strategy, with devastating consequences. Strange as it may seem, I see little difference in broad principle between his attempts to avoid feeling bad and the measures that are widely adopted by millions of people every day to maintain the myth of feeling good. Such measures appear to reduce the stress but do not address the real issues.

Hugh Mackay describes the current overemphasis on feeling good as an obsession with happiness.[9] He is particularly concerned about what we are doing to our children when, out of concern for their self-esteem, we try to maintain them in a state of continual happiness – when we constantly praise them as if everything they do is wonderful, and do our best to ensure they never hear a word of criticism or correction.

> Instead of helping them cope with such trials as a cranky teacher, for instance, or perhaps with a teacher who doesn't seem sufficiently obsessed with the self-esteem of her every charge, we're down at the school, kicking up a fuss ...'I want them to be happy,' we say, as if we believe perpetual happiness is not just a worthwhile goal but also the birthright of every child.[10]

Within a conceptual framework appropriate to their age, it is important that we allow our children to experience all normal facets of their lives. We are short-changing them if we deny them 'those precious formative experiences of disappointment, deprivation and failure'.[11]

However, exposure to reality obviously needs to be matched carefully to the age and circumstances of the child. It is incongruous that many parents who feel they must protect their children from potentially painful realities about themselves and life, nonetheless allow them to be exposed to horrendous 'virtual' situations in movies, TV programs and computer games.

Facing reality

Associated with the current focus on self-esteem is what Hugh Mackay describes as a 'mad cult of perfectionism sweeping the upper middleclass':

> You've encountered it, I'm sure: friends who are obsessed by the need to get their children's (or their own) teeth straightened, their thighs sculpted, their breasts or their backyards professionally redesigned ... They want the perfect career trajectory, the perfect holiday, the perfect pesto, the perfect latte, the perfect eyebrow, the perfect orgasm ... They yearn for perfect politicians (ha!), perfect banks, perfect cars, perfect shoes, perfect kitchens ... our new angst springs from the discovery that our lives are falling short of some crazy ideal of perfection clogging our minds like a cancer ... Nothing is perfect. Life is messy. Relationships are complex. Outcomes are uncertain. People are irrational.[12]

For almost everyone, life is an experience of both sunshine and shadow; anguish, pain, and even despair are all part of human existence. Mackay points to the benefits of allowing ourselves to grow through pain and describes happiness as 'a kind of euphoria – pleasant in short bursts but hardly a rich enough resource to sustain us through life's vicissitudes'. Viktor Frankl, a Viennese psychotherapist and Holocaust survivor, described the ability to deal well with unavoidable suffering and death as 'a witness to the uniquely human potential at its best'.[13]

The following quaint words, penned some 150 years ago by the monk Hugo Bassi, seem pertinent here:

> Measure thy life by loss instead of gain;
> Not by the wine drunk, but the wine poured forth;
> For love's strength standeth in love's sacrifice;
> And who so suffers most hath most to give.

And this often-quoted poem is saying much the same thing:

> I walked a mile with Pleasure,
> She chattered all the way,
> But left me none the wiser,
> For all she had to say.
>
> I walked a mile with Sorrow,
> And ne'er a word said she;
> But oh, the things I learned from her
> When Sorrow walked with me![14]

I used to say, 'I don't want to talk to anyone who has not suffered because they usually have nothing to say.' That may be overstating the case, but my experience has been that those who have encountered disappointment and tasted failure are the wiser for the experience if they rise above despair and confront their situation appropriately.

> *One of the wisest counsellors I have ever known had been a prisoner of war at the notorious Changi prison during the Second World War. While he was lying immobilised in the concentration camp after horrific injury, a colony of meat ants took up residence in his leg. They ate the gangrenous flesh away and saved his life. I sought him out at a point of crisis, and anger at betrayal, in my own career. He asked if I was disillusioned. 'Of course,' I replied. Then he said: 'Deal with your illusions about the perfection of even your friends. You can only suffer disillusionment if you first are suffering from*

The You-Must-Feel-Good-Look-Good Myth

an illusion!' *Profound wisdom from one who had experienced a reality check through his suffering.*

If we invest our lives in creating a bubble of perfection to avoid pain, then we are heading for disillusionment. Sometimes feeling 'bad' or uncomfortable is the appropriate response to our circumstances; our challenge is to learn to deal with these feelings in healthy and authentic ways.

> *A friend told me of a business associate who was dismissed from his senior position through downsizing. He was well short of retirement age, but unlikely to find appropriate employment offering similar status in his highly competitive industry. Every day for many weeks, he took his briefcase and left early, apparently pursuing his usual work routine. The family suspected nothing and carried on spending as usual – all on credit, of course.*
>
> *The debts piled up – private school fees for his children, expensive cars, mortgage payments on his luxury home, good living, credit card interest. Daily pub Scotch to cover his pain only added to his problems. Then the bomb dropped. The house went. The cars were repossessed. The children had to leave their private schools. His wife moved on, unable to cope with the change of lifestyle and her loss of confidence in her husband's credibility. Were it not for a group of men inspired by faith and compassion, meeting specifically to offer support to people in his situation, it is very likely he would have joined the growing ranks of businessmen who have opted out of living.*

Self-esteem mythology does not have the answers when we face difficulties such as these. Somehow, we need to find the resilience to cope with living in the real world. Yet the extremes to which contemporary society goes in order to try to shield the individual from sadness and failure may actually undermine their ability to persist and master difficult situations.[15]

US civil rights leader Martin Luther King Jr, who eventually sacrificed his life for his cause, wrote: 'The ultimate measure of a man is not where he stands in moments of comfort and convenience, but where he stands at times of challenge and controversy.'[16] One of the often unsought by-products of triumphing over physical, social and personal obstacles is a sense of happiness and fulfilment, which may or may not be the same as what is called self-esteem.

Looking good

Many men and women give a high priority to looking good, and expend inordinate amounts of time and money on trying to achieve this goal. This includes spending not only on clothes, hair care and beauty products but also on a whole range of purely cosmetic procedures now offered by dentists, surgeons and beauticians. Such efforts are met with varying degrees of success and, all too often, disappointment. The fact is that most people are unlikely to achieve the classic good looks they crave, no matter how much money they spend.

More than 43,000 cosmetic surgical procedures were carried out by members of the British Association of Aesthetic Cosmetic Surgeons in 2012, predominantly breast augmentation and eyelid surgery. In the USA that year, nearly 15 million surgical and nonsurgical cosmetic procedures were performed. Breast augmentation also headed the surgical list there, while Botox anti-wrinkle injections, fillers and chemical peels were popular non-invasive cosmetic treatments.[17]

When it was reported that Australians spent $1 billion in 2010 on cosmetic procedures, outspending the USA on a per capita basis, the President of the Australian Psychological Society suggested that perhaps, instead of shrinking wrinkles, Australians should be seeing shrinks![18] While women account for the majority of such procedures throughout the world, many men are also lining up for tummy tucks, removal of 'man boobs' and surgery to alter facial features. I have even come across a few misguided preachers and religious groups on cable TV who exhort women to spend big dollars on Botox and cosmetic surgery, in order to fulfil beauty expectations and be sexy for their men.

Some years ago, American TV host Larry King interviewed aesthetic plastic surgeon Dr Robert Singer, chair of *New Beauty*'s Editorial Advisory Board. While this magazine does provide a service by informing the public about various procedures and the dangers of rushing into cosmetic surgery, it also effectively promotes the industry. When asked why people have Botox treatment when it can give them such a dead-pan look, Singer gave the absurd response, 'Because they want to look natural.'

When questioned about the morality of being part of the fast-growing commercialisation of the physical appearance improvement, Singer replied, 'We live in a competitive age. It [cosmetic surgery] gives a competitive edge.' Sadly, there may be some truth in this statement. A recent article, describing an international trend towards increased marketing of cosmetics to males, laments a proven bias towards good looks for men in the job market and in commercial dealings, and a general preference for employing those with a youthful appearance.[19] Women continually struggle against such bias.

Has our society really become so obsessed with physical appearance that higher cheekbones, a straighter nose or fewer wrinkles can override executive skills, trade or professional competence, administrative ability and technical savvy when we apply for a job?

Shaping our children

There is ongoing controversy about the way some parents push young children into beauty pageants, sometimes with terrible consequences.[20] We read of young teens being encouraged to have expensive cosmetic surgery before their bodies have matured. Padded bras have even been manufactured for girls who are still in infants' school.

Concern is increasing about stress in children caused by the pressure to look good. The following excerpt from a 2013 government review of cosmetic intervention in the UK does nothing to allay this concern:

attitudinal research suggested younger people see cosmetic procedures as a commodity – something they might 'get done'... This can be attributed in part to the use of social media and the growth in celebrity culture: 41% of girls aged 7 to 10 and 62% aged 11 to 16 said they felt some pressure to look the way celebrities do.[21]

Doctors are now treating eating disorders in children as young as six and seven who are already beginning to feel pressured to be thin.[22] A university study of 11–14-year-old children of both sexes revealed that almost 80% were worried about their body shape. Half of the boys and 78% of the girls wanted to be smaller, yet only 23% were actually overweight. These findings were attributed to the fact that both girls and boys are being given a dangerously distorted perception of what a normal body looks like. The often digitally enhanced body shapes presented to them by the media are completely unattainable.

Our children are now also intensely fashion and brand conscious. Nearly half of the world's urban 8–12-year-olds believe that the clothes and brands they wear describe who they are and represent a crucial aspect of achieving social acceptance.[23] In a market-driven pop culture that links building self-esteem with looking and feeling good in the right brand names, parents whose incomes limit their ability to comply fear their children are being disadvantaged and embarrassed because of their relative poverty.

Some time ago I came across an outstandingly attractive book for children entitled *The Lovables in the Kingdom of Self-Esteem*.[24] It troubled me, because I saw it as very good in many ways, yet also very dangerous because of its potential to implant self-esteem mythology in young children. One character, Pierre Peacock, celebrates and boasts of his beauty as an expression of his positive self-image. He finishes his self-description with the observation that 'true beauty comes from an inner glow'. But for some children, the bulk of his pronouncement is more likely to lead to despair than hope. When he

The You-Must-Feel-Good-Look-Good Myth

says, 'I am beautiful ... My feathers are beautiful as can be. I spread them wide for all to see', what is he saying to the ugly duckling?

Observing and admiring someone's beauty is one thing; giving the impression that magically it can be yours is another matter altogether. It is fine to tell the child who is not blessed with good looks, or who suffers from obesity or a disfiguring illness or injury, that beauty is *inside*. But it is counterproductive to use the peacock to illustrate this point. He is a striking example of beauty on the *outside*, which may never be attainable for these children.

I can identify with children who are not the peacocks of this world:

> *As a child, I was accidentally doused with boiling water and spent months in hospital, suffering excruciating medical treatments. Burn treatments were more primitive in those days and the resultant scars gave me considerable doubts about being beautiful. I knew all the clichés – your beauty is on the inside, and so forth – but, even back then, there was considerable societal pressure to look good.*
>
> *It was not a mantra telling me something I couldn't believe that helped save me from despair. It was the acceptance of Glena, the woman who was to become my wife. When she first saw my scars, she didn't pretend they were attractive or beautiful. She simply reached out, tenderly touched my damaged arm and said gently, 'Oh, you poor guy.'*

Glena's loving acceptance of me, scars and all, and her loyal support over more than 40 years of marriage, have done more for me than any cosmetic surgery or self-esteem-boosting formula could ever have achieved.

4

The Boosting-Self-Esteem-Brings-Happiness Myth

Many who live the feel-good, look-good lifestyle see happiness primarily in terms of success in the physical, external world. It is about making good progress in your chosen career – about money, status, power and peer recognition. A wide range of techniques aimed at boosting our self-esteem are on offer, with claims that they will help us move towards success and happiness. High self-esteem, success and happiness thus seem inextricably linked.

This is not the view of psychologist Martin Seligman, an expert in the field of psychological health who has written extensively about self-esteem. He is sceptical about many reports of apparent correlations between high self-esteem and success, and low self-esteem and failure. He raises the question: how do we know whether it is low self-esteem that is causing failure, or failure that is causing low self-esteem? His conclusion is that self-esteem itself seems to cause nothing at all; rather it is 'the whole panoply of successes and failures in the world' that influence our self-esteem.[1]

An article that put a large dent in this chapter's myth was published about ten years ago by USA psychology professor Roy Baumeister and his colleagues.[2] It provided an in-depth evaluation of the assumption that high self-esteem produces positive outcomes, based on the results of all relevant studies available at the time.[3] Baumeister was initially a supporter of the self-esteem movement, but had become concerned about the deficiency of hard evidence to support its claims.

Baumeister's team did find that self-esteem scores (having a positive view of oneself) and measures of happiness (life satisfaction) were linked, but, as already mentioned, this does not necessarily mean that high self-esteem *caused* the happiness. More importantly, they found no evidence that benefits were produced through self-esteem-boosting measures, whether therapeutic interventions or school programs. What is more, they said, 'our findings do not support continued widespread efforts to boost self-esteem in the hope that it will by itself foster improved outcomes.' In fact, they expressed concerns about this practice. Baumeister was later reported as saying that his findings were 'one of the biggest disappointments of his career'.[4]

Those of us who live in affluent Western societies do have plenty to be happy about. We have enormous freedom to go where we want and do what we want, whenever and with whomever we choose. Of the vast array of goods and experiences that advertising tells us will bring happiness, all but the most expensive are accessible to the majority.

How happy should the well-heeled, well-medicated, well-entertained, well-fed, well-clothed, well-housed, well-informed person of today be? If happiness can also be enhanced by adopting pop-culture techniques aimed at boosting our self-esteem, as the myth suggests, we should surely be the happiest people who have ever lived. The truth is that on the whole we are not.

How happy are we?

Happiness is an elusive quality, hard to define and hard to measure. We can use the word in a trivial sense to describe the transient emotion we experience when enjoying a pleasurable activity. In a recent market research 'happiness survey' reported in the media, almost three-quarters of the 'Gen Y' respondents – that is, people born between the late 1970s and late 1990s – reported finding happiness in watching TV or eating comfort food such as chocolates, biscuits and pizza, while more than half found happiness surfing the internet.

While such enjoyable experiences may be an aspect of happiness, my focus here will be on a deeper appreciation of the term. At this deeper level, happiness is better described as a mood or disposition rather than a transient moment of pleasure – as an ongoing state of wellbeing, contentment and satisfaction with life.[5] There is ample evidence that this kind of happiness is not guaranteed by material wealth, nor by the high self-esteem thought to be associated with it.

In a TV interview during a visit to Australia in 2009, Martin Seligman was asked, 'Are people happier today than they were 30 years ago?'[6] He responded by referring to studies of 52 nations in which changes in happiness have been assessed directly. He said that happiness went up (albeit slightly) in 46 of these, it went down in 5, and in 1 (Australia) it was unchanged. He emphasised that in Australia happiness had not increased, despite more than 15 consecutive years of economic growth and improved living conditions for the majority. 'If one has a belief that happiness is a function of economic growth,' he said, 'people in Australia ought to be out there leading the world [in happiness], but they're not.'

Gregg Easterbrook, after thoroughly reviewing research on the issue of global satisfaction in 2004, concluded that:

> The percentage of Americans who describe themselves as 'happy' has not budged since the 1950s, though the typical person's real income more than doubled through that period. Happiness has not increased in Japan or Western Europe in the past

half-century, either ... Far from feeling better about their lives, many are feeling worse.[7]

Particularly significant in this context is an extensive 25-year study of 60,000 people, published in 2010, which provides strong evidence that 'prioritising success and material goals is actually harmful to life satisfaction'.[8] The iconic lament of the Rolling Stones in their 1960s song – '(I Can't Get No) Satisfaction' – seems even more pertinent today.

Among the many reports of celebrity millionaires who are sad, lonely and unfulfilled, the story of Austrian tycoon Karl Rabeder makes for a refreshing change. He divested himself of his business and luxury possessions, choosing instead to live in a bedsit on about $1400 per month, with proceeds going to a charity he had set up in Latin America. 'Money is counter-productive – it prevents happiness,' he said. 'I had the feeling I was working as a slave for things that I did not wish for or need.'[9]

I do occasionally meet the aggressively self-interested high flyer who professes to be happy on purely materialistic grounds, but I have found this to be rare. On the other hand, I have met many people who seem to be happy despite a lack of material abundance.

> *While travelling through Arizona, my wife and I had a memorable encounter with Amerindians of the Hopi tribe. The Hopi are a retiring people who have lived in the canyons of the rivers in a deeply contemplative relationship with nature. The community we met lived, hidden from tourist view, on the top of a series of tall mesas, the steep-walled plateaus that are common in the area. At that time, by choice, they were living without electricity or any connection to the technological society not far away.*
>
> *After chatting with a waitress in a roadside eatery, we were invited to visit this community during a weekend of special dancing and feasting. Through our experiences during the hippy days of the 1960s and 1970s, we had developed a deep respect for some of the values of indigenous cultures, including our Australian indigenous culture. On this occasion, Glena and I settled*

> ourselves on the roof of one of the low adobe dwellings. Hour upon hour, the dancing continued. It was a highly emotional experience for us.
>
> Sitting next to us on the roof was a woman in her mid-thirties, dressed in stylish Californian fashion. It was clear that she was Amerindian. She told us that she too was Hopi. We sensitively broached the subject of the anomaly between her urban appearance and her obvious connection to this local community. This was her explanation:
>
> 'Today I have come home. I am the former CEO of a Silicon Valley corporation in the IT industry. I have left behind me a high-paying position, a luxury car and upmarket housing, and all that goes with a successful Californian lifestyle. I have resigned from my company and I'm not going back. I do not want my children destroyed as those of the world I have left behind so often are. I want community and tribe – not an endless supply of unnecessary and useless things.'

This is, perhaps, an extreme example – and yet, such a story is completely consistent with the findings of scholarly research described above. The truth is that all the trappings of success and the good life do not in themselves guarantee happiness and satisfaction.

An 'epidemic' of depression

In simple terms, it is reasonable to say that a person who is suffering from clinically diagnosable depression is not happy, as the following description illustrates:

> While we all feel sad, moody or low from time to time, some people experience these feelings intensely, for long periods of time (weeks, months or even years) and sometimes without any apparent reason. Depression is more than just a low mood – it's a serious illness that has an impact on both physical and mental health.[10]

Severe depression completely disrupts a person's life. As well as withdrawing from once-enjoyed activities, they may experience hopelessness, a lack of interest in others, suicidal thoughts, and eating, sleeping or sexual dysfunctions.

The incidence of clinical depression therefore offers insight into the level of unhappiness within a particular society. By 2003, Gregg Easterbrook's research had led him to conclude that 'throughout the United States and the European Union, incidence of clinical melancholy has been rising in eerie synchronization with rising prosperity'.[11] At about the same time, Australian researcher Clive Hamilton was expressing his concerns about an incongruous social malaise, which he referred to as 'affluenza'.[12]

> Despite their affluence, the citizens of rich countries are no happier at the beginning of the twenty-first century than they were fifty years ago. This is the great political fact of our age. If high incomes, the object of so much determined effort, fail to improve our wellbeing, then why have we striven so hard to be rich? ... Do we live in societies peopled by autonomous, creative, contented individuals living harmoniously in their communities? The answer must be 'no' ... The proliferation of psychological disorders in rich countries over the last five decades is a testament to this.[13]

Hamilton lists as outcomes of affluence: drug dependence, obesity and loneliness, as well as psychological disorders ranging from depression, anxiety and compulsive behaviours to a widespread but ill-defined 'anomie' (a state of alienation).[14] 'Depression characterises contemporary consumer society,' he says.

Martin Seligman has described what is happening as an 'epidemic of depression' occurring in Western culture.[15] In contrast to the 1960s, he says, when depression was a fairly unusual condition typically occurring in middle-aged women, 'Depression has become the common cold of mental illness and it takes its first victims in junior high school – if not before.'[16] He is convinced that 'there is more depression now than 30 years ago, particularly among young people.'[17] I believe many of his peers would agree with him. However, trying to measure the extent to which depression has increased over the years turns out to be a complex issue, about which even the experts hold differing views.

Complicating factors include variations in criteria used for diagnosing major depressive disorders over time and by different researchers, increasing public and professional awareness of such disorders, increasing social acceptance of mental illness and increasingly aggressive marketing of anti-depressant drugs.[18] Seligman, while acknowledging that there is now controversy about whether the escalation in the prevalence of depression deserves the appellation of 'epidemic', offers the following summation of current thinking: 'All of us in the field are dismayed by how much depression there is now and how much of it goes untreated.'[19]

Clinical 'non-polar' depression is now recognised as a major scourge of contemporary Western societies, despite all the apparent benefits available to their citizens. The World Health Organization estimates that depression will be the number one health concern in both the developed and developing nations by 2030.[20] By 2001, depression mixed with anxiety was already the most common mental disorder in adults in Britain, with almost 9% meeting criteria for diagnosis.[21] In Australia, depression ranks as the third highest of all diseases in terms of its total impact and the highest cause of non-fatal disability.[22] One in seven of the current population will be affected by this condition at some point in their life.

As I have travelled abroad in recent years, I have seen headlines in the press in the UK, New Zealand and the USA, as well as Australia, bemoaning the new phenomenon of primary school children needing weekly visits to an analyst to deal with their depression. It is now one of the most common mental health problems in young people.

A US national survey of more than 13,000 college students in 2004 indicated that nearly 45% were so depressed that they had difficulty functioning, while 94% reported feeling overwhelmed by everything they had to do.[23]

Today's schoolchildren [in the USA] are at a higher risk for depression than any previous generation. As many as 9% of children will experience a major depressive episode by the time they are 14 years old, and 20% will experience a major depressive episode before graduating from high school. Having suffered from depression as children, these young people are much more vulnerable to depression as adults.[24]

American psychologist Jeanette Twenge, after analysing data from more than 50,000 college students and children, has reported increasing rates of anxiety, as well as depression, among what she terms 'Generation Me'.[25] She subsequently reported a six-fold increase in depression in high school and college students in the USA between 1938 (the era of the Great Depression) and 2007.[26] There was a five-fold increase in anxiety and other mental health issues over the same period. All the students surveyed completed the same standard test.

Alongside the cost in terms of human suffering, escalating depression imposes a serious economic burden on society as a whole. With this disorder now affecting so many young people, not just those who are abused and marginalised, we might expect to see increased investment in dealing with this issue from all possible angles. However, my impression is that more money is going into developing new drugs for dealing with symptoms than into research aimed at identifying and addressing possible causes.

Feeling self-sufficient and sure of ourselves might be a great advantage while things are going well, but it is not enough to ensure survival when life becomes difficult. Many young people who lost their jobs during the recent economic crisis were shattered, because they had been taught that their strengths and abilities would ensure they could always achieve their goals. They really believed the catch-cries: the world is your oyster, you can be whatever you want to be.

Pumping up our self-esteem without reaching for a bigger-than-ourselves life raft may temporarily keep us afloat, but it will not be long before we find ourselves floundering. Clinical depression, which may develop when life turns sour, is typically associated with feelings of hopelessness (that is, a lack of meaning or purpose in life) as well as a sense of worthlessness. In Seligman's experience, more is gained in therapy by helping such a patient become active and hopeful, rather than by focusing on their low self-esteem.[27] Richard Eckersley also sees hope as vital. He suggests that hope can easily be lost because of the often episodic nature of contemporary life, and its lack of coherence and predictability.[28]

The ultimate unhappiness

> *In the 1990s I travelled to Switzerland to participate in a Conference organised by Moral Rearmament (now known as Initiatives of Change). This was attended by a diversity of people, including representatives of two notorious and rival street gangs in the USA: the Crips and the Bloods. One of their leaders said to me, 'In the inner city we kill each other in the battle to survive, but in the 'burbs the kids kill themselves.'*

Most of us would regard suicide as the ultimate expression of unhappiness. Some years ago my own organisation, through links with the Australian Bureau of Statistics, gathered Australia-wide data about suicide deaths for every year from 1950 to 1998.[29] The data suggested that a boy aged 15 years in 1998 would have a 1 in 100 chance of dying by suicide before his 44th birthday. It also revealed an alarming, progressive increase in the annual rate of suicide among people aged less than 40 years. The suicide rate for those aged 15 to 29 years increased more than two-fold. A similar increase in the overall youth suicide rate between 1950 and 2003 was reported in the USA.[30]

An interplay of many complex factors underlies this phenomenon, which is happening among young people generally, and it is not limited to those who are socially or financially disadvantaged.[31] Increasing individualism may be a major contributor, as well as the promotion within Western societies of 'a cultural norm of personal freedom and control that is unrealistic, unattainable or otherwise inappropriate, resulting in a gap between expectations and realities'.[32]

> *One of my closest friends in years gone by was an ambulance officer, a man of integrity with a high sense of social responsibility. He frequently shared with his trusted friends the confronting and distressing experience of being called to suicide situations. His years of responding to such calls convinced him that suicide had little to do with wealth or poverty. In fact, in his experience, the typical young adult male committing suicide was economically well off.*

Being financially secure does not provide immunity against depression and suicide. As Jesus of Nazareth said long ago: 'Life does not consist in an abundance of possessions.'[33]

Why do we feel dissatisfied?

It would be wrong to conclude that the self-esteem movement is in itself the sole cause of the high levels of dissatisfaction and the concerning rates of depression, anxiety and suicide in Western societies. The causes are complex, as there are numerous aspects of contemporary living that may undermine life satisfaction. They include:[34]

- the unsettled nature of progress. Progress allows some problems to be truly solved, such as the eradication of smallpox, but often in solving one problem a new one crops up. For example, we can now travel anywhere in the world, but we have to deal with the resulting problems of energy consumption and its environmental impact
- an active preference for bad news. News organisations love the word 'crisis' and use it as often as possible: highly speculative bad news is given considerable coverage, while confirmed good news is barely reported. The media create an impression of a country that is getting worse by focusing on smaller and smaller risks, missing the larger point that big

risks are in decline
- we suffer 'choice anxiety'. We are burdened by the vastness of options that confront us, from buying groceries and clothes to deciding which mobile phone or internet provider to use, how to invest our money or our next travel destination. Yet we also suffer 'abundance denial' – that is, we somehow manage to convince ourselves that we are deprived of material comforts in the midst of plenty
- a blurred distinction between needs and wants. Most people throughout history have had to order life around needs in order to eke out an existence. Today, when millions of people rarely lack anything in the needs category, the wants can become insatiable.

Other possible contributors are the speed and extent of change, enabled by advances in technology and information sharing.[35] Our increased connectivity can result in high levels of stress and anxiety. Overloaded and overwhelmed by the volume of the input we receive and the multiplicity of competing demands for our attention, we may find ourselves longing for the relentless bombardment to stop. Daniel Sieberg, a former science and technology correspondent for CBS and CNN, suggests that we may need to 'detox' our digital life, and has offered some interesting suggestions for achieving this.[36]

Despite all the advantages it offers, modern life has become relatively insecure. Many now live with a sense of imminent danger, either real or media-induced – climate change, terrorism, criminal activity, financial ruin and so on. Our work environments are also becoming less secure. The average person may now go through half-a-dozen or more strategic shifts in occupation or retraining, often accompanied by relocation and isolation from family support systems. Many workers feel pressured to be available electronically 24 hours a day in order to protect their jobs, which comes at a cost to health and relationships. The powerlessness engendered by unemployment, or employment without just reward or long-term job security, is often more damaging than the actual financial hardship entailed.

Coinciding with the increasing complexity and perceived insecurity of our lives is a waning of what Seligman calls the 'commons', or 'spiritual consolations' – things we could fall back on in the past for support in hard times, such as a belief in the nation, in God, in family and community, or in a purpose that transcends our lives.[37] Having a religious belief into which one's life fits with meaning is a far greater buffer against dissatisfaction, dejection and anxiety than many other solutions. But this 'belief' needs to go deeper than simply being religiously inclined and having emotional and social attachments to church, synagogue or mosque.

Sociologist Richard Eckersley has commented that in any other culture, at any other time, we would be telling our children stories that would help them construct a worldview and cultural context, to help them define who they are and what they believe, and give them the fortitude to cope with life.[38] Bemoaning the fact that this was no longer happening, he wrote of a survey conducted by *The Sydney Morning Herald* in 1990 in which 120 bright, normal, healthy 11-year-olds were asked to write down their perceptions of Australia's future. The newspaper reported being astounded at the depth of the children's fear of the future and their bleak predictions for their nation. Given this finding, it is concerning that many of our children are now frequently exposed to scenes of horror, devastation and strife via the media.

Seligman sees clinical depression (the most widespread form of depression) as culturally rather than biologically induced: my likelihood of suffering depression has much to do with how I see the world, my expectations about my life, its meaningfulness or meaninglessness, and my social networks or lack of them.[39] He also believes 'modernity' makes people much more vulnerable to clinical depression.[40] Much youth depression seems to be undergirded by this difficult-to-categorise lack of substantial worldview, or confusion about meaning or purpose in life.

Relationship breakdown is a further contributor to depression. Anecdotal evidence we have gathered through Concern Australia, over our many years of conducting high school Values4Life seminars (formerly Christian Option seminars), consistently indicates a strong link between youth mental health and the breakdown of romantic and other significant relationships. Warring parents is another major factor.

In acknowledging the multiplicity of factors that may contribute to escalating rates of dissatisfaction, depression and suicide, it would be a mistake to let the complexity blind us to the growing evidence that self-esteem mythology is playing a part. For example, Seligman believes that the 'bloated self', pumped up by self-esteem teachings that foster individualism and grandiose expectations, is fertile soil for the growth of depression. He writes:

> When we find ourselves helpless to achieve our goals, we suffer depression. The more I believe that I am all that matters and the more I believe that my goals, my success, and my pleasures are extremely important, the more hurtful the blow when I fail.[41]

Ten years ago in England, I voiced my concerns about self-esteem-related issues in an address to several thousand young people at a large Greenbelt Youth Festival. While at that time my ideas were less developed than they are now, the basic message was a snapshot of the content of this book. At the end of the session, I was set upon quite aggressively by two 'youth counsellors', who asked whether I realised how much damage I had done to young people in the audience who had low self-esteem. In contrast, my key message received an enthusiastic response from the young attendees: life would be more liberating if they were to look beyond their obsessive focus on themselves and their self-esteem. Some told me it was a huge relief to them. They felt as though the self-esteem emphasis of their counsellors, rather than helping them, had actually entrapped them in a cycle of dependence and depression. Feedback I received later indicated that this presentation had been a pivotal point in the life of one young man, who over time made a remarkable recovery from depression.

Food for thought

One of the most emotional experiences of my life occurred in the 1980s in the mountains of El Salvador during civil war in that country:

> *Through human rights action, members of our organisation and others had helped secure the release of a Lutheran bishop imprisoned for showing solidarity with the poor. After his release, he took our small multinational group on a walk through the mountains to a refugee camp and faith community linked to the American Lutheran church.*
>
> *The community comprised mainly women and children, because so many of their men had been killed in the civil war. Some were the wives and children of men who had been tortured and executed by the brutal, dictatorial military junta. They were without any means of defence.*
>
> *Their housing consisted of black polythene plastic sheeting draped roughly over the branches of trees. There had been rain a few days before, and they had managed to fill an old 44-gallon fuel drum with water. We saw a small girl dribbling one jam tin of this water over her naked body with a look of ecstasy on her little face – her first chance to have a primitive shower in weeks.*
>
> *Just prior to our visit, a military helicopter had landed on the top of the hill where these people lived. The community were asked to identify their Bible teacher. Religious leaders, including martyr Archbishop Oscar Romero, had been slaughtered in considerable numbers, because their theology taught solidarity with the poor and non-violent resistance against oppression. The courageous teacher identified himself and was taken away to become one of the many who 'disappeared' during this terrible time.*
>
> *During this encounter, the soldiers also asked what provisions they had. They replied innocently they had little else but a small store of measly*

corncobs. The soldiers took almost all of the corn, saying that this food could be used to feed rebels. When we visited, I was taken to see the small cache of corn they had been able to hide in the bush. The average corncob was so sparsely populated with grains that it would not even be fed to hogs in affluent rural communities.

Shortly before we left, we were invited to share with them a celebration meal, as a token of gratitude for our courage and solidarity in coming to visit. Of course, our courage had been minimal. We snuck in and out with the bishop and flew back to our democratic safety zones within a few days. But it was clearly important for us to respect their cultural values by accepting their hospitality before we left.

They made tortillas for us using their meagre remnants of corn. They baked them in small mud ovens, adding a few other odds and ends – maybe some meat captured from the bush. They had no idea where food would come from in the weeks ahead. We overfed Westerners, knowing their situation, ate as little of their dwindling resources as courtesy allowed – we were all close to choking on each morsel.

Tears flowed as these amazing people spoke of their lost loved ones, yet they were able to sing their religious songs from the heart, accompanied by a cheap guitar. They even joked and told stories of lighter, happier moments. Our impression was that they were at peace, despite living life in these extreme circumstances. Their faith and love were palpable.

These people did not have a weekly therapy session, and yet they seemed to have some of the healthiest psyches I had ever encountered. Faith, enduring hope and shared love and community were their sources of mental health. Depression and suicide seemed totally incongruent. We, on the other hand, required a day of debriefing by experts following our disorienting experience. We were traumatised!

The real issue is this. These people had none of the things my television tells me I must have to live a good and happy life. Despite this, they exhibited qualities in the most adverse of circumstances that somehow insulated them from depression. To them, the status of their self-esteem was not even a consideration. In their world, people die from starvation. They seek food for their families. We, with our overfed bodies and bloated opinions of ourselves, feed on the myth of self-esteem and remain emotionally undernourished.

5

The All-About-Me Myth

Now that the constraints of socially imposed roles have weakened in rich countries, oppression based on gender, class and race is disappearing. The daily struggle for survival has, for most people, been banished. We have entered an era characterised by individualisation, where for the first time in history we have the opportunity to 'write our own biographies', rather than have the chapters foretold by the circumstances of our birth.[1]

Much of the progress towards individual freedom is welcome. Yet from it has grown an increasing trend towards self-obsessed individualism, one that I believe is against our very nature as human beings. This is not in our best interests as individuals or as a society. We are social animals wired for communal relationships, not for isolation of the ego. A person wrapped up in themselves is not only a very small parcel but also a very vulnerable one.

I would argue that in the search for self, to the detriment of interpersonal relationships and a sense of community, we in the West have reduced, rather than enhanced, our innate possibilities. If we can break free from the shackles of self-obsession, we can find a

The All-About-Me Myth

much more fulfilling, socially connected and meaningful life.

Many influences in our society encourage us to believe the destructive all-about-me myth. These include not only the direct input of self-esteem-focused motivational presenters and writers but also the marketing strategies of commercial bodies, who have opportunistically exploited this myth as a means of increasing profits.

Sometimes, however, unhelpful ideas are communicated with the best of intentions. For example, one of the judges of the Australian TV series *MasterChef*, in a well-meant attempt to encourage a contestant who was being eliminated from the competition, offered the following counsel: 'Whatever you choose to do, it has to be for you, something that makes you happy – not anybody else, just you. It's the right advice in life.' It is true that some people may need encouragement to be more independent when making choices, but adopting this recommendation as a general principle for life could be disastrous. As Richard Eckersley points out, we are in trouble when 'thinking *for* ourselves' becomes redefined as 'thinking *of* ourselves'.[2]

What we need is not individualism, but a deeper understanding of individuality and 'personhood', expressed within the context of community and relationship.

Free to be me

In 1987, I attended a World Congress in Amsterdam focused on global Christian communication. A seminar was held to provide information and enable dialogue about the special difficulties faced by religious practitioners and communicators under repressive regimes. The presenter Walter Smythe described a meeting with a number of dissident Czechoslovak students and young people, whose Christian faith was at the core of their brave resistance.

They pressed him about the attitudes of American youth. Were the young people of America more unselfish and committed to moral values? Were they more committed to the betterment of the lives of their citizens than the young people he had met in their country? Smythe had to admit that their own sense of commitment and self-sacrifice far exceeded anything he had seen in his

> own country, even among those who claimed to be committed people of faith. They were shocked by his honest reflections on the widespread selfishness, materialism and lack of guiding moral principles of American youth. With a sense of amazement bordering on despair, they replied: 'Then why, sir, do we fight for freedom?'

Obviously, this story is not meant to be interpreted as a basis for non-resistance to tyranny. However, it does challenge us to reconsider the whole notion of freedom – not only national freedom but also individual freedom.

A key aspect of the all-about-me myth seems to be the goal of having untrammelled freedom to do as I please, when I please, regardless of the wishes or needs of others and the consequences of my actions on them and wider society. This attitude echoes libertarian thought as expressed in the writings of John Stuart Mill. He argued that liberty promotes individuality and that individuality is 'one of the leading essentials of well-being'.[3]

I question whether those who embrace the all-about-me myth are really as free as they think they are. Strangely, self-esteem mythology tends to restrict freedom by applying intense pressure on the individual to conform to certain ideals. We can find ourselves being pressured subliminally to live, dress, speak, earn, relax, travel and even relate to others according to certain stereotypes of success and happiness. Never before has individuality been so celebrated or pop-culture conformity and coercion been so all-pervasive.

> In the Values4Life program presented by Concern Australia in high schools, we would sometimes ask an entire senior class to join us in shouting 'I'm an individual', to be followed by two loud grunts while punching the air with their fists. We continued repeating this routine with increasing volume and energy until, eventually, the chanting became as one voice yelling, 'I'm an individual'. We, the leaders, would then stop, fold our arms, look at them, shake our heads in amazement and then start laughing. One by one the more astute students would recognise the absurdity of the situation. Here they

were, mindlessly conforming to their classmates in a statement affirming their own individuality! Soon the entire class would be grinning sheepishly as they realised what was happening. From this point, we would talk them through the current culture of pop conformity and its incongruity with their desperate yearning to establish individual identity.

Such conformity is reinforced by the media at large, under the guise of encouraging individual freedom, with slogans such as *express yourself, do your own thing, the choice is yours*. Here is Clive Hamilton's summation of the situation:

> Entrenchment of personal and political freedoms in Western societies has been responsible for the atrophy of true individuality, especially under the impact of consumer capitalism and neoliberal politics since the early 1980s. Modern consumer capitalism encourages conformity, one-dimensionality, and an intolerance of those who seek to break away from the expressions of individuality manufactured by the market.[4]

Hamilton goes on to argue that the paradox of modern consumer life is that we are deprived of our inner freedom by our very pursuit of our own desires. His deep exploration of this issue has taken him to the unexpected conclusion that we cannot be truly free unless we commit ourselves to a 'moral' life.

Market-driven 'independence'

A distinct separation of teenagers from their parents' culture, known as the generation gap, has become the norm in Westernised societies. It is widely regarded as an essential part of developing healthy individuality and self-esteem. This gulf has proved a bonanza for entrepreneurs, who clearly have an interest in sustaining and widening it. The marketing of many unnecessary items is now aimed at teenagers, as well as increasingly younger target groups (labelled 'tweens', 'tweenies' or 'tweenagers'), purportedly to help them forge identity and freedom. Teenage and tweenage pop-culture is now a mega-billion-dollar concern. The notion of a generation gap is also actively reinforced by the pronouncements of pop psychologists and other ill-informed media 'experts' and sociologists.

The advice columns of many magazines are of little help to distressed parents seeking advice about dealing with the generation gap. In a weekend magazine, I read a letter submitted by a troubled mother asking the advice of three 'experts' (a sociologist, a media star and a journalist). She was concerned that her pre-adolescent daughter, in response to youth-targeted advertising and media pressure, wanted to dress like Britney Spears. Should she say no to the sexy outfit she wants?[5] All three commentators responded that it was none of the mother's business. Besides which, the child was simply seeking to develop her own individuality and enhance her self-esteem. There was not a hint that there may be another way of dealing with the issue.

In this example, and in many other situations, the underlying assumption seems to be that it is a universal, biologically and psychologically driven imperative for all children to shock and worry their parents by behaving outrageously. It is as if rebellion and developing an all-about-me attitude are an essential rite of passage and a natural precursor to appropriate self-esteem.

Anybody with even a modicum of education in cultural anthropology knows that this is not true. Tribal groups generally have no such separation between children and parents. Typically, a child at about twelve years of age leaves the circle of childhood playmates, undergoes rigorous ritual processes and education to prepare them for the responsibilities of adulthood, and then takes their place on an equal footing with the adults of the tribe. (Of course, in saying this I am not implying blanket approval of every practice associated with such coming-of-age rituals, past or present.)[6] Usually, the elders delight in the growing prowess of the young people; the young people appreciate the mentoring and experience of the tribal elders. In this way, mutual care and respect are nurtured.[7] While the emphasis in patriarchal societies is on the initiation of males, there are parallel processes for females.

This principle is not limited to so-called primitive tribes. The Jewish culture's ritual of Bar Mitzvah serves to introduce the thirteen-year-old boy into the adult world. At this age he is regarded as capable of knowing the difference between right and wrong, and of being held responsible for his actions. He takes on the responsibility of doing as much as he can to learn the obligations he will have as an adult and is granted the right to participate as an adult in religious services. This ceremony represents a significant stage in a lifelong process of learning religious and cultural values from the elders of the community.[8]

A devastating consequence of the generation gap in our Western societies is that successive generations, separated from the elders of their 'tribe' and cut adrift as vulnerable isolated entities, artificially create risky temporary tribal groups, comprising similarly inexperienced and vulnerable youth, in a quest for identity and freedom. My contention is that, to function effectively as a society in which individuals are free to live happy and fulfilling lives, we need the energy, enthusiasm and creativity of youth functioning hand-in-glove with the tribal wisdom of the elders.

Me-focused sex

In the 1960s, the freedom afforded to youth by contraceptives created a revolution in beliefs about sexuality. Historically, sex had been primarily about producing children, as well as social survival and the transmission of values from one generation to another. It now seems to have become a leisure and spectator sport. Increasingly, under the influence of the all-about-me myth, happiness and sexual gratification are being sought by detachment from relational demands or limitations. The irony is that, to be experienced and enjoyed fully, sex needs to be *relational*.

It is not only Christians who believe that relationship with the other participant is an important aspect of sex. Jewish psychotherapist Victor Frankl has also weighed in on this debate. Here is a summary of his views:

> Many confuse sex with love. Without love, he [Frankl] says, sex is nothing more than masturbation, and the other is nothing more than a tool to be used; a means to an end. Sex can only be fully enjoyed as the physical expression of love. Love is the recognition of the uniqueness of the other as an individual, with an intuitive understanding of their full potential as human beings. Frankl believes this is only possible within monogamous relationships. As long as partners are interchangeable, they remain objects.[9]

Because this rings true for me, I have sought to deal with this issue in the Values4Life seminars presented by Concern Australia in high schools. It may surprise many readers that such ideas are received with overwhelming enthusiasm. Many students express great relief that someone has been willing to introduce this point of view.

> *Some years ago, a young woman exited hastily from one of our Values4Life seminars in a flood of tears. Here is the gist of the explanation she gave us: 'The other day I got drunk at a school party. I had sex with a guy I didn't even know. When I sobered up I was devastated and went to my mother for help. We are a single parent family. I said to my mother tearfully, "Is sex for human beings the same as two dogs doing it on the nature strip? Have I just become an animal or something?" My mother replied, "Your grandmother was a horny [expletives omitted] and your dad and I screwed around. That's why our marriage broke up. I guess it's just in our genes. Just take precautions – roll over and enjoy it." I went to my mother for advice and that's all I got.'*

The distress of the young woman was not over the possibility of an unwanted pregnancy or infection with a dread disease. Nor was it fear of a male's abuse. It was concern that her personhood was in question in the context of meaningless and relationless sex. She had not yet been brainwashed by the view that sex is all about my achieving the most sensational orgasm. Intuitively, the teenager knew something her mother had forgotten – there is more to human sexuality than instant gratification.

Sexual activity is not a purely human pursuit, of course. Frogs do it. Snakes do it. Hippos do it. The urgency and the pleasure are there, at least in higher life forms. What is not there in other species is that which defines our identity as humans. When a dog is on heat, nature rules. I remember well the extreme precautions we had to take when our poodle was ready to mate. Every male dog in the neighbourhood tried to climb, burrow under or destroy the fence in an attempt to be part of the action. However, as human beings, we have the capacity to choose in even the most sensuous and inviting situations. We can choose to say *yes*, *wait* or *no*, for all kinds of social and moral reasons. It is not our capacity to be aroused sexually that makes us human, it is our ability to choose to deal with this arousal according to our social, moral and spiritual orientation and values.

In the area of human sexuality, many individuals are already short-changing themselves, in terms of their potential for maximising sexual fulfilment, by choosing the instant gratification option. Self-esteem mythology's unbalanced emphasis on individualistic feel-good experiences has undoubtedly played a part in this. Unless we wake up to what is happening and react accordingly, the present flawed understanding of sex will continue for generations to come.

Me-focused 'altruism'

The party-time of Western self-gratification has become like an analgesic that deadens the human conscience to the depressing global reality of obscene levels of poverty, disease, and hunger around us. Some individuals respond generously to appeals for donations when catastrophic disasters strike in their own country and beyond, but for the most part we turn inwards in self-absorption rather than take up the far more challenging – and fulfilling – issue of eliminating the causes of world poverty and disease.

The celebrated generosity of a handful of billionaires, giving what is in reality a trifling proportion of their vast wealth to humanitarian causes, can help us avoid facing our own disconnection from the suffering of others. I recall the flurry of activity in 2005 when rock stars put together a huge global concert, *Make Poverty History*. People were frantic to obtain tickets. It is a sobering commentary on our age when unprecedented starvation and poverty in the vast continent of Africa raises minimal interest unless it receives the attention of celebrities, many of whom may otherwise be living extremely self-indulgent lives.

Recently, in a doctor's surgery, I picked up a magazine that focused on the lives of the rich and famous. There was an account of a film star visiting villages in Africa and announcing to the world her profound concern for its people, accompanied by a photograph of her own accommodation during the visit. The latter was sufficiently opulent to meet the requirements of a millionaire on holiday in the Pacific – an incongruity that seemed to be lost on both the reporter and the celebrity. In the cultural garden patch, the wholesome cabbages of compassion can become smothered by the weeds of wealth obsession.

Handouts from the world's billionaires are sometimes labelled 'conspicuous philanthropy'. Not only do these gestures make the donors feel good about themselves, they also generate very favourable publicity, all at little real cost. After all, if you have a billion dollars, a 10-million-dollar gift to a worthy cause will not place any appreciable restrictions on your lifestyle. I wonder how much would be given if donations were to be made anonymously, without personal kudos or psychological gain for the donor.

These words of St John Chrysostom, written in the fourth century, remain an apt reminder of the injustice of lionising those who have the financial means to give conspicuously:

> The amount we give is not judged by the largeness of the gifts but the largeness of our hearts ... When a rich man makes a large gift ... he is heartily thanked; and although he will not feel the lack of money, he is praised for generosity. When a poor man makes a small gift, nothing is said; even though that gift may cause him to go hungry, no one praises him or thanks him. It would be better to praise no one than to confine our praise to the rich.[10]

For some very wealthy people, tax relief may be the motivation for giving money away. Others are perhaps driven to do so by an awareness that they are, to much of the population, objects of criticism and jealousy. Well-publicised acts of generosity will help build their image and increase their popularity. We encounter glaring examples of celebrities whose misdeeds are forgiven almost overnight by the public because of such largesse. When their unfaithfulness towards their families or propensity for targeting vulnerable women is exposed and vilified, they set up a generous foundation to assist a children's hospital or some other worthy cause, as if their tax-relieving generosity absolves their poor moral and social behaviour.

Philanthropy is also tarnished if the financial empire capable of giving so generously is built on any form of exploitation or injustice. Wealth can be acquired by fair means or foul. Some employers and corporations have attained an unbelievable level of wealth by imposing policies that have kept thousands on minimum wages, condemning them to a life of ongoing struggle, and in appalling working conditions. Recently, the plight of low-paid clothing workers in many countries was highlighted when a defective clothing factory block in Bangladesh collapsed killing more than 1000 workers.[11]

> *I once had the disturbing experience of slipping into an Egyptian sweat-labour factory, where small children were working extended adult hours,*

making massive carpets of the style advertised at bargain sales in my own country. Their remuneration was bare survival.

Throughout the Western world, the increasing casualisation of the workforce leaves families without sufficient, reliable income to cover the ever-spiralling cost of living, and without sickness benefits, sick leave, superannuation, and annual holidays.

In the late 1990s, the USA government took Microsoft co-founder Bill Gates to court, alleging corporate malpractices that contravened monopoly laws. Shortly before that happened, I remember seeing a TV interview in which Gates quite boldly announced that he had every right to his financial empire and had no intention of scattering his gains to the needy. In fairness, I must add that Gates has since changed his tune. He has established foundations to support medical research, education and AIDS prevention, and has recently announced that most of his billions will go towards defeating poverty when he dies. *Time* magazine has celebrated him as the greatest philanthropist in history. That change of heart is certainly praiseworthy, whatever the reasons for it. Perhaps Gates reached a point where he realised that one thing he really wanted – the admiration and love of his fellow human beings – could never be attained through aggressive market success. And perhaps that is a worthwhile reason to shift from corporate oppressor to human benefactor.

For many people, not only celebrities, it is inconceivable to do something just because you believe it is the right thing to do. Admittedly, discerning the 'right thing' becomes difficult if we lack value systems and worldviews against which to measure our actions. The question 'what's in it for me?' has become a widely accepted guide to choosing the right course of action: it's the all-about-me myth in another guise.[12]

Genuine, other-focused altruism does exist, of course. Many wealthy, powerful people have toiled sacrificially for the great benefit of others with little regard for personal reward. Jimmy Carter, former President of the USA, is a good example. He failed to produce a magic economy for America, but he set his sights on a great vision: to bring peace between Egypt and Israel – a classic attempt at reconciliation of historical antagonists. The Peace Accords he helped to forge still hold, more than 30 years later. Using the vast resources of his government, he also set out to eradicate preventable diseases such as smallpox and guinea worm. The first goal was achieved in 1979, the second is now within reach.

In retirement, President Carter and his wife committed themselves to *Habitat for Humanity*, giving weeks every year, despite advancing years, to construct houses for the poor. For them, hankering after self-esteem-boosting popular acclaim does not seem to be an issue. Such a focus is simply too small a package to excite people to go all out for a larger vision.

Whatever the motivation for doing good, human beings seem to be hardwired to feel good when they do good. However, it is a chicken-and-egg case of which comes first. Do you seek to *do good* for its own sake, which may well generate *feeling good* as a natural consequence, or do you follow a motivational mantra that says *go and do some good because it will make you feel good*?

Living in relationship

Proponents of the all-about-me myth often feed their audiences impressive quotations that encourage forging ahead in isolation from others, such as, 'The best place to find a helping hand is at the end of your arm'.[13] Of course, it becomes a problem if you have both arms amputated, figuratively or literally. You may just need somebody else's hand. The following ancient wisdom makes more sense to me: 'Two are better than one ... If either of them falls down, one can help the other up. But pity anyone who falls and has no one to help them up.'[14]

In the early 1970s, our then fledgling group (now Concern Australia) was known for a somewhat countercultural stance on war and materialism. However, we had a greater reputation as a caring, creative organisation. This news spread quickly and dissident young people flocked to us, along with people who had special needs.

An urgent phone call came from friends of mine in New Guinea, missionaries who were out of their depth, not knowing how to respond to a young woman who had dropped out of university and arrived on their doorstep in a state of deep depression. In anguish, they recounted the crisis. Taking a glass tumbler, the girl had placed it on the kitchen floor and stomped on it with her bare feet, grinding the splintered glass into her flesh.

She was sent to us in such a state of mental collapse that her self-inflicted injuries did not appear to generate normal responses to pain. She frequently self-mutilated by pressing burning cigarette tips into the tender flesh of her breasts. Her degree of false guilt and self-loathing was such that she said to us one day, 'At least if I'm sinful, I'm something.' If ever there was a classic case of what we now label low self-esteem, this girl was it. She was not the subject of sexual abuse. She was not without networks of friends. She was not eking out an existence on the street. To all intents and purposes, she was a normal person whose sense of self was fractured.

Today, hopefully, a person exhibiting such extreme behaviour and distress would be referred to professional help for diagnosis and appropriate treatment. However, agencies that could respond to crises such as this were yet to evolve. In the years that followed, she was to find total healing through community and the live-in care of one of our pastors and his wife.[15] Of even greater significance, I believe, over this period she was surrounded by love and acceptance in our somewhat alternative community. Her recovery certainly was not achieved through anything like the current self-esteem-directed dictums.

Eventually, she was incorporated into the loving family of a Uniting Church minister and his wife. She is now married with children and has become so healed psychologically that, for many years, she and her husband

and family have been committed to the demanding task of caring for marginalised people.

Legion are those who would testify that in times of difficulty it is not good to be on your own – those who have found loving and willing hands to help when they needed them. I believe that the *feeling good* we experience when we help others is not mainly about enhanced self-esteem. It reflects the satisfaction that comes from affirming we are social animals who need each other. Life is not all about *me*. It is about *us*. It is about expressing our uniqueness in the context of relationship with others. Dennis Kinlaw, a historian and respected Christian author, writes:

> Persons never come alone. The concept of the person as the autonomous individual whose identity is found in the self is an Enlightenment notion that finds no support in reality ... The concept has no roots in the original definition of person. The modern search for a self in isolation is futile. We moderns have an imperfect understanding of what it means to be a person. We do not understand that persons find themselves in their relationships; therefore, we do not understand what it means to be ourselves.[16]

For this reason I prefer to use the term 'personhood' rather than 'self', as does Kinlaw. Self seems such a lonely word to me, whereas personhood embraces the notion of neighbourhood. It encapsulates the African saying, 'I am, because we are' – I am defined, not by my self alone, but also by those to whom I belong in love and mutual commitment. Among most tribal cultures, the conversation starter is not likely to be 'Where do you live? What do you do?' but rather 'Who are your parents, grandparents, brothers and sisters, aunts, nephews, cousins?'

The following story offers a stark reminder of the ultimate emptiness of self-absorption.

> It was the annual corporate motivational gathering of the largest insurance corporation in the Southern Hemisphere. The massive Trade Centre in Melbourne was awash with highflying sales and managerial leaders. The conference organisers insisted I ride my new Harley Davidson up the aisle to the podium between thousands of delegates before giving the keynote address.
> Despite an enthusiastic introduction, I was far from relaxed or confident. I had been given a daunting task. I had been asked to present a holistic view of life, weaving corporate business, personal pleasure, life ideology, family and recreation into one seamless, successful life garment. At the conclusion of the address, I quoted the famous words of Jesus Christ, 'What good is it for someone to gain the whole world, and yet lose or forfeit their very self [personhood]?'[17] I spoke about the importance of balancing our me-focused pursuit of financial gain and material possessions with our family lives, with adequate time for caring communication and the nurture of relationships. Because my address cut right across the prevailing obsession with financial success above all else, I was very surprised when the audience gave me a standing ovation.
> Later, a conference executive said to me, 'You can't know how poignant and appropriate your words were. The guy who received the top sales award today is a man determined to make every post a winner. He works day and night to pursue every available client. Recently he told us of a conversation with his wife. She had pointed out that, although the family had every material provision they could ever need, they hardly ever had his time or attention. He turned to his wife and said, "It's your birthday tomorrow. When your new luxury car is delivered, that should shut your mouth." He even boasted to his peers that immediately after this conversation, having finished his evening meal, he grabbed his brief case and went out to make another corporate killing. His wife wept.'

Many would agree that material prosperity is no guarantee of good relationships or compassionate, caring family life or even ultimate satisfaction. Having said that, neither is extreme poverty. A wise king once prayed to God that he would not be so poor as to be driven to crime for survival, nor so wealthy that he would be blinded to the things that matter most.[18]

The value of community

Because, by very definition, a self-esteem focus tends to isolate the individual, the prevailing strong emphasis on self-esteem flags that we have already become a radically individualistic society. We teach our children to compete, almost to the exclusion of co-operation or community consciousness. Cut loose from communal restraint, individuals are easy pickings for forces of corruption, irresponsibility and greed. I agree with Martin Seligman: the human ego is too fragile to survive even the mid-range pains and failures of real life alone, and the collapse of support provided by historic institutions such as extended family, community and church has left us even more vulnerable.[19] Our belief systems and our relational context have an enormous effect on our mental health.

Richard Eckersley is another who recognises the limitations of all-about-me individualism:

> While loosening social ties can be liberating for individuals and create more dynamic, diverse and tolerant societies, too much cultural flexibility can have the effect of trivialising the convictions and commitments that we need to find meaning and to control our own lives. Tolerance, taken too far, becomes indifference, and freedom abandonment. Our power as a people comes from a sense of collective, not individual, agency; from pursuing a common vision based on shared values, not maximising individual choice in order to maximise personal satisfaction.[20]

Social connectedness and reinforcement of values and meaning come through tribal solidarity, family, religious affiliation or other shared-values groupings. In a culture lacking these, therapy often steps in to fill the gap. I recall a scene from the movie *Crocodile Dundee*. When told someone was going to an expensive analyst for their weekly therapy session, Dundee asks, 'Hasn't he got any friends?' I realise this response is oversimplistic, and I acknowledge the value of appropriate therapy when needed, but there is much more to Dundee's light-hearted comment than many would recognise. The cry for intimacy, love and meaning in relationships will never adequately be met by therapy sessions alone. A supportive community is invaluable, ideally comprising at least some people who care about us enough to be honest with us, even when the truth is hard to take.

Some anthropologists have noted that highly technological societies tend to be weak on the plane of relationships. In Western societies, the wealthy and important person who is surrounded by adoring friends is often rejected and forgotten when the fortune is lost. The words of this old blues standard are true now more than ever:

> Once I lived the life of a millionaire
> Spending my money, I didn't care
> I carried my friends out for a good time
> Buying bootleg liquor, champagne and wine
> Then I began to fall so low
> I didn't have a friend, and no place to go ...
> It's mighty strange, without a doubt
> Nobody knows you when you're down and out.[21]

Some years ago, political scientist Robert Putnam showed that social bonds are the most powerful predictor of life satisfaction.[22] Supporting this conclusion, a recent survey of 136,000 people in more than 130 countries has established that the experience of happiness or wellbeing on a day-to-day basis depends on social and psychological factors, rather than material prosperity.[23] Key social factors identified included being treated with respect, and having friends and family to turn to in an emergency. Sadly, in some urban locations in our societies, a neighbour could be dead for weeks or even months before anyone checks to find out why they have not been seen. In more relationally oriented communities, such people would be known and included in mutual care.

> Years ago, at the time of economic collapse in the Soviet Union, my wife and I were part of a team who were taking essential items of medicine, food, and other basics to Eastern Europe. We visited Yugoslavia just after Tito's death, when street fighting was beginning in a few areas. We visited Bulgaria, where we gave writing pads and ballpoint pens to an Orthodox priest, who sobbed because he had not been able to purchase such items to prepare his sermons for his congregation. We visited the Ukraine, where a peasant woman wildly gesticulated to us, obviously requesting aid. She refused our offer of money – money couldn't buy what she needed. What she wanted was our shoes and some of the clothes we were wearing.
>
> We visited Romania within weeks of the fall of Nicolae Ceausescu. The open doors of capitalism seemed to have delivered an abundance of cheap Western porno movies, which were being hawked on the streets, but you couldn't buy a banana or an orange. While walking the back streets of Sibiu on 'Resurrection Sunday' during their celebration of Easter, we met a group of Gypsies. These Romani people are no strangers to rejection but they were particularly loathed in Romania at that time. There were unfounded insinuations that their relative prosperity resulted from some clandestine deal with Ceausescu's regime. The group we met swiftly befriended us. Wherever we went, people seemed to sense that we genuinely cared about marginalised people.
>
> Each family in this community had carefully nurtured an item of livestock – a goat, a sheep, a pig or a fowl – during the previous year, in preparation for this one special day on which the resurrection of Christ is celebrated. We were invited to join them in their joyous feasting and the drinking of their homemade cherry-plum wine. One man, who was fluent in English, took us to his home, which was a large, ancient American car in a rundown shed with a makeshift cooking area in one corner.
>
> To our surprise, hanging from the front corner of the shed was a tatty American flag. He explained: 'We lived in New York. I had a good job there.'

I said, 'Why on earth would you return from a good job in New York to live in a country that is in such a state of political chaos?' He replied, 'I saw the beginnings of the impact of American television on the values of my children and the cohesion of my family. I would rather live on a pittance here, where we care for one another and hold on to our family values, than have all the so-called benefits of American materialism.'

This encounter unsettled me and made me wonder about the inherent superiority Western technological societies espouse. Here was a cultural cohesion long gone from my Western tradition. My wife and I had experienced the same sense of community among the Hopi Amerindians in Arizona (see chapter 4). During their festivities, we had seen old men with withered skin and bent frame, dancing alongside sweet children and robust young men and women. Relationships excluded no one. Subtle respect crossed all generational barriers. What is more, at least one member of each of these communities, having been given the opportunity to embrace the Western cultural model, had fled back to what we would regard as a lesser lifestyle – for the sake of community and greater enduring values.

6

The Never-My-Fault Myth

This myth may not be a recognised catchcry of the self-esteem movement, but it is an almost inevitable consequence of its teachings, especially the feel-good myth. When we make a mistake or realise we have contributed to the collapse of a relationship or project, the natural response is to feel bad, not good. We may feel humiliated, ashamed or remorseful. We should also expect to feel bad (if we are psychologically healthy and in touch with our emotions) when we deliberately act in ways that are in conflict with our moral and ethical values. This means that, in such situations, we have to either allow ourselves to feel bad or, in a misguided attempt to protect our self-esteem and continue feeling good, delude ourselves into believing that we have not done wrong or behaved irresponsibly.

Mistakes happen

An English satirist of a bygone age got it right when he said, 'To err is human.'[1] The reality is that mistakes and failures are a normal part of human existence. I am deeply concerned that unrealistic aspirations and self-assessments, driven by self-esteem mythology, are pushing us in the direction of being unable to own our mistakes appropriately.

Trying to live by the whatever-you-want-to-be myth can become a trap in this respect. If we not only set unrealistic goals for ourselves, but also hold fervently to the belief that they are achievable, it may become difficult for us to own our failures and admit that we are not living out our dreams perfectly. In the same way, if we believe that one of the secrets of succeeding in life is to experience only pleasant, 'positive' emotions, we will be strongly motivated to deny uncomfortable feelings. We will also be tempted to conceal our weaknesses from others to ensure we retain their good opinion.

The only way we can keep on feeling good when things go wrong is to avoid admitting to ourselves or others that we have made a mistake or been part of the problem. I see the biblical advice to think of ourselves with 'sober judgement' as a far better option.[2] This means acknowledging our strengths and our weaknesses, our successes and our failures, and the ways we hurt others intentionally or otherwise.

We need to learn how to fail well. As Seligman points out, 'If you think of the thing in your life that you're most proud of, your greatest success, it was almost certainly something that involved a large number of sub-failures, each one of which you had to do something to overcome.'[3] Adults need to fail, children need to fail, and we all need to allow ourselves and each other to experience the associated 'negative' emotions. If we impulsively protect ourselves from personal responsibility, we miss out on opportunities to learn persistence skills. The same is true for our children.

Children need to learn that failure is not the end of the world, and to build confidence through solving problems. Here is a summary of suggestions offered by child psychologist John Irvine, known to many Australians through his books and appearances on TV:[4]

- don't always protect your children from life's lessons for fear

of hurting them. Let them experience failure and gain confidence from beating problems
- don't deliberately let your child win when you play games with them. This can build an unrealistic expectation that they will never lose, making it hard for them to cope when life or mates teach them otherwise
- if they fail at a particular task and want to give up, just leave it be, or break it down into smaller steps so they can find their own way to success without your intervention
- children are more likely to work hard, try hard, do their best and enjoy life if they enjoy learning, if they see it's okay to make mistakes, and if they enjoy the sense of growing their 'brain muscle'.

In similar vein, *New York Times Magazine* recently published a substantial article entitled 'What if the secret to success is failure?', which described the character-building benefits when teachers allow their students to deal with failure.[5]

A sign of emotional health and maturity is being able to accept ourselves as fallible human beings, while continuing to do our best to avoid mistakes. If we own our mistakes when they happen, we can make amends and learn from them. When dealt with appropriately, our mistakes and failures often do lead to positive outcomes. At the very least, they provide a valuable correction to fanciful beliefs that we are infallible or have sufficient resources in ourselves to beat any obstacle.

Guilt can be good

We know that pain serves a good purpose by protecting us from behaving in ways that are potentially damaging to us. It is less widely recognised that appropriate guilt can serve a similar purpose. Just as there is nothing bad about feeling good when you are doing 'good', there is nothing bad about feeling bad when you are doing 'bad'.

I believe one of the tragedies of our current society is that we are becoming increasingly bereft of social and moral awareness.[6] Many people have managed to virtually obliterate the psychic pain that ideally accompanies wrongdoing – what we might call twinges of conscience.

A sense of right and wrong, often referred to as our conscience, is innate in all humans (except for those suffering certain forms of psychological illness, brain damage or intellectual impairment). This is an inbuilt human capacity to feel uncomfortable when the line of perceived appropriate behaviour is crossed. It may manifest as guilt, remorse, anxiety, defensiveness, anger, fear of rejection and so on. What we discern as right and wrong is socially informed, however, and shaped by the society around us.

It is possible for us to be conditioned to think things are bad when they are not. It is, of course, equally possible for us to be socially instructed in such a way that destructive, selfish behaviour becomes acceptable as good. In such a context, we may not experience an unpleasant reaction to such behaviour, even though it is demonstrably not good for us, our fellow citizens or our society. In this respect, I believe our culture today is seriously endangered.

> *My personal belief is that there are some universal truths, even if only a few. I believe that, whatever our culture, we should regard every fellow human being as having significance equal to our own. I believe we should recognise that love is the highest virtue to which a human being can aspire. By that I mean transcendent love – unconditional, other-focused, self-sacrificial love – as distinct from mere sexual intimacy or a warm, fuzzy feeling. I believe that we should experience a pang of appropriate guilt and feel bad when we are doing the wrong thing – that is, acting in ways that are violating these ideals.*

Nature itself has prepared us, as social beings, with complicated biological and psychological warning systems that kick into action not only when we are in physical danger but also when our lives are out of sync with appropriate human behaviour patterns. Quite apart from any religious viewpoint, it simply makes sense in terms of human survival for us to be hardwired to behave in ways that promote co-operative communal existence. Martin Seligman writes:

> Anxiety, depression, and anger have long evolutionary histories in which they're trying to tell us something. Depression, feeling sad, tells us we've lost something. Anger alerts us to trespass, anxiety alerts us to danger. All of these messages, by their very nature, carry pain, and it's this pain that makes them impossible to ignore and goads us to get rid of them. They're an alarm system, they're not a flawless alarm system, they're very often wrong, but insofar as we jump in and try to dampen the system, we can lose the message ... about how our commerce with the world is going.[7]

We must of course avoid the pitfall of transferred, false or inappropriate guilt. False guilt may be imposed on us by others who express their judgement of our behaviour, often to manipulate us to do what they want. It also arises from defective social conditioning under the influence of people (or regimes) who have misinformed us about moral issues or damaged our sense of self, intentionally or otherwise. Such false guilt needs to be exposed and denied.

Just as for pain, the ability to feel guilt can be regarded as a gift, provided that it is an appropriate response to our actions. Habitually sweeping our guilt under the carpet may make us feel better in the short term, but it will have disastrous consequences for us in the longer term. I need to be clear here, however, that I am not advocating wallowing in our guilt or feeling unendingly ashamed of ourselves. Rather, we should be responsive to guilt, allowing our psychic pain to redirect us to a healthy resolution of guilt, and into better moral and social patterns of behaviour.

How, then, do we resolve our guilt? Many people think that religion is heavily into the *guilt* business. My preferred worldview option, Christianity, is often pilloried for being hung up on sin and guilt.

While this may be fair comment when applied to some periods of history and even to some Christians or churches today, it is a sad misinterpretation of the genuine faith movement that sprang from the life, death and teachings of Jesus Christ. It is not healthy to live in a state of perpetual guilt, any more than it is to live in pain. Living with guilt is like living with an arthritic soul.

I like to say that Christians are in the *forgiveness* business. Nobody thinks you are a fool if you name a disease and follow up by offering a cure for it. As I see it, Christianity does just that: it looks squarely at the issue of guilt and offers hope of resolution and a way forward. It recommends a process that is healthy for anyone: assess the situation realistically, take responsibility for your part, acknowledge when you are wrong, make amends where possible, make changes where appropriate and learn to forgive those who have wronged you.

The blame game

In response to reports and comments about the death of a 15-year-old boy after a schoolyard fight at a high school in Australia, a parent sent a letter to the editor of a major newspaper.[8] In it, he decried the way that Generation Y students were adopting a never-my-fault attitude, blaming the principal, the teachers, the school – anyone but themselves – when, in reality, it was the students who had started the fight. He suggested that perhaps the only 'fault' of the parents was that they had overindulged their children to such an extent that they did not believe they were responsible for their actions.

This is not only a Generation Y issue. Human beings have always been very good at shifting the blame. The classic story of Adam and Eve, which predates written history, observes this human failing very shrewdly. When Adam and Eve succumb to the temptation to eat the one forbidden fruit in the Garden of Eden, and are then called to account by God, Adam blames the woman for making him do it, while Eve blames the serpent who tempted her.[9]

My contention is that the blame game, which has always been

with us, is being exacerbated by the myth of self-esteem. Now more than ever, people are under pressure to shift the blame elsewhere, either consciously or unconsciously, rather than taking personal responsibility. I read of a cyclist who, while illegally using a dedicated bus transit lane, viciously attacked the driver of a bus who overtook him. Although the cyclist was clearly at fault (he was the one who was trespassing in the bus lane), he turned his wrath on the bus driver who was simply going about his business.[10]

Another way we can attempt to sidestep responsibility is by blaming our behaviour on issues from our past. Sometimes when talking to old-timers who have experienced the rigours of the Great Depression of the 1930s, war and concentration camps, I wonder how we can be so fragile over the imperfections of our lives. For most of them (as for many in the world today), feeding, clothing, housing and caring for the kids was an all-consuming occupation. There was no time for trawling through the past. As basic survival has become easier for us in the West, we have acquired the dubious luxury of having more time to indulge in self-focused thinking and activities.

There are some people who do genuinely need attention and therapy for damaging experiences in their past, such as childhood abuse or other seriously traumatic events. I understand and accept this. For many people, however, the desire to blame behaviour on trivial experiences from the past and the imperfections of even good parents has become a convenient cop-out. Excessive dwelling on the past can propel us into a false belief that we are helpless victims of our past, and can rob us of the incentive to change.

Reviewing the past is not in itself a problem; remaining helpless victims of the past is. Seligman is emphatic that, while we may be affected by the past, we are not its prisoners.[11] When therapy is needed, he advocates a forward-looking approach that takes our problems here and now and helps us work on them, while encouraging personal responsibility for change. Perhaps it is in part a false sense of imprisonment by our own past that motivates us to seek obsessively to engender both self-esteem and freedom in our children beyond all realistic expectations.

As a society, we have become amazingly adept at sidestepping our responsibility. Michael Lallo's comments hit hard:

> Eat too much? You don't lack self-control; you have a 'disorder'. Your shopping addiction is the result of work stress. And thanks to your partner's lack of communication, you couldn't help but have an affair.[12]

Pick up any newspaper and you are likely to find at least one example of this kind of blame shifting. Sometimes it presents as an individual's defensive reaction but, especially in the case of cultural idols, others may step in to shift the blame. If a footballer can prove, or even if he makes the claim, that his orgy with a half-drunk young groupie was consensual sex, the newspapers rise to his defence by claiming he was wrongly charged and is completely innocent. If he is married, the opinions or feelings of his wife are of little social interest unless she leaves him. Even then, his hero status is barely dinted.

The serial unfaithfulness of international golfing champion Tiger Woods, something for which he himself issued a seemingly contrite public apology, was excused in the press by the unsubstantiated claim that he was a 'sex addict'.[13] It's not his fault. It's just the way he is – it's in his genes. Another well-known sportsman's mobile phone indiscretions became legendary. The iconic status of the celebrity, rather than being diminished, often seems to be enhanced by such revelations.

I am deeply concerned when I read that perpetrators of antisocial and even criminal acts have become overnight celebrities on social networking sites, receiving thousands of supportive comments. In many situations it now seems as though 'the people who criticise wrongdoers are the sinners, while the wrongdoers themselves are simply "being human".'[14]

Another largely unrecognised but far-reaching consequence of the blame game is an upsurge in frivolous or vexatious litigation. It clogs our courts, costs taxpayers money and unnecessarily delays hearings of more significant matters. Frequently, such cases result in gross miscarriages of natural justice, achieved by clever exploitation of loopholes in the law. Anyone who stays in touch with the news is sure to have come across such cases. Here are just a couple of examples:[15]

> *A man sued a cinema owner because he fell on the stairs as he was leaving and injured himself. The truth is that he had chosen to leave before the lights were turned up, while the credits were still rolling at the end of the movie. One of his claims against the owner was that the stairs were extremely ill lit!*

> *While I was in the UK, I read about a florist who had run a small business on the concourse at Marylebone Station for many years. She was taken to court by a man claiming £1.5 million in damages, for neck and back injuries he suffered when he allegedly slipped on a petal from her stall. He won the case; the florist was facing ruin.*

While it is true that the stall owner had previously been warned to keep her stand clear of hazardous waste, surely the injured party also had a responsibility to take reasonable care. In any case, as outraged readers commented, there was no evidence that the offending petal actually fell from her display. What if someone had purchased the flowers before the petal fell? Sometimes accidents happen that are nobody's fault.

Responsibilities and rights

Taken to its natural conclusion, the end product of the myth of self-esteem is a hedonistic and highly individualistic society. Ultimately, it becomes all about me, about my doing whatever it takes to make me feel good and keep me feeling good. By very definition, this pleasure-based life has to be devoid of feeling guilt, shame, embarrassment or concern about our actions, or about our failure to consider the needs of others. It also has to be devoid of taking responsibility, in so far as that risks bursting our feel-good bubble.

One of the dominant features of an individualistic society, as opposed to a community-oriented society, is an emphasis on individual rights rather than responsibilities: rights in the market place; rights in relation to marriage, divorce or partnerships; children's rights against parents; minority rights and so on.

I sincerely believe in human rights and have often found myself called upon to stand with those whose rights are being abused. My toughest experience of this happened in the Philippines in 1989, when I found myself arrested and under sentence of death for defending the rights of rural peasants.[16] However, a sense of personal rights needs to be balanced by a philosophy of social responsibility. Otherwise, it is very likely that people will refuse to take individual responsibility for their choices when they turn out badly. Instead, they may become highly indignant and proactive in response to even trivial events they perceive as infringements of their rights. Free democratic societies are particularly vulnerable to this antisocial behaviour, which is an aspect of the never-my-fault and all-about-me myths.[17]

Our ability to take personal responsibility is also influenced by our ability to recognise and acknowledge when our behaviour is inappropriate. This, as we have seen, depends at least to some extent on our cultural conditioning. A male chauvinist society does not promote shame among males who are overbearing and exploitative towards women: rather, it often transfers the guilt to women. Similarly, an individualistic society does not promote a sense of responsibility for one's personal behaviour and its effects on others. Nor does it promote communal responsibility or encourage the acts of selflessness that are intrinsic to a well-functioning society.

In a healthy society, people are prepared to act beyond self-interest: the parent takes personal risks to protect the child; the whistleblower courageously denounces practices that are detrimental to the company or the welfare of others. When viewed from this perspective, sidestepping responsibility seems a rather pathetic attitude, more likely to damage than boost self-esteem.

Social critic and columnist, Barbara Ehrenreich, uses the term 'bubble-itis' to describe the condition in which people become caught up in self and success to such an extent that acknowledging responsibility is off the radar.[18] She writes about the USA financial services firm Lehman Brothers Holdings Inc., whose disastrous collapse during the global financial crisis was precipitated by greed-based mismanagement and excessive risk taking. Astonishingly, after the real estate bubble burst, the attitude of the CEO appears to have been, 'What could I have done differently? … How did it all go so disastrously wrong?'[19] Even people of extraordinary talent and extensive experience can become so blinded by self-justification that they cannot see the consequences of their actions until catastrophe occurs.

Common sense tells us that having a never-my-fault attitude is unhealthy behaviour. Indeed, I see it as analogous to a neurosis – a tragic impairment that severely hampers our ability to experience life in all its fullness.

7

Gurus of the Myth of Self-Esteem

The term self-esteem was virtually unheard of in the popular media until the 1990s. Now, it permeates popular culture and professional discourse. It seems to have developed into something of an obsession, causing relatively healthy individuals to invest their money in books, downloads, DVDs and self-improvement courses in the search for personal perfection, success, happiness and peace.

When I walk into newsagencies and bookshops, I am appalled to see how many popular books are authored by a handful of self-appointed gurus. They further their financial empires by writing yet another book, often holding out the promise of success as the drawcard. As Hugh Mackay observes:

> All over the country, we have been hearing the merchants of self-esteem flogging their suspect merchandise. Where did this lopsided emphasis on self-esteem – self-regard, self-importance – come from?[1]

This emphasis creates a very profitable market for what I call the gurus of the myth of self-esteem. Among them are pop psychologists,

Gurus of the Myth of Self-Esteem

motivational experts and lifestyle coaches, as well as spiritual practitioners. Many of these appear genuine in their belief that they are responding helpfully to an expressed need, but I suspect that far too many are opportunists who simply want to make a fast buck. Unresearched, unverifiable solutions to the supposed problem of under-inflated self-esteem are multiplying in our consumerist society. I fear for the long-term mental and moral health of my own and other nations if the distorted messages about self-esteem currently being disseminated remain unchallenged.

Media gurus

The living image via TV can be used to powerful effect. It is no longer the case that seeing is believing: now, with the capacity to exert virtual wizardry via digital manipulation of images, seeing is deceiving in many instances. In addition, the juxtaposition of images during TV interviews enables a larger-than-life presentation with maximum emotional impact. Camera angles and cheering audiences assist in producing the desired effect. Most of us are well aware of the potential for this kind of manipulation, but in a feel-good society, the tendency to get caught up in the emotion of the moment often outweighs our motivation to analyse the content.

We are exposed to a surfeit of prosperity motivators like Anthony Robbins, Bob Griswold and Paul McKenna who, for a price, will share the secrets of their phenomenal success. They may offer them via TV (replete with a cheering, adoring audience), a costly personal appearance or a suite of products. Naturally, they do not tell us about the majority of their devotees who never achieve millionaire status.

The failure of a particular guru's formula to produce the desired outcome may simply keep people coming back for more, thereby ensuring the coffers of said guru are kept nicely filled. How easy it is to blame those who fail – you didn't follow the instructions completely, you didn't truly believe you could achieve your goals. If the success formulas presented were as foolproof as claimed, the world would be suffering a surfeit of millionaires.

The adrenalin rush evident in the enthusiastic audiences displayed on TV is sufficient to keep the self-esteem junkie hooked on the concept. The histrionics of the presenter – racing up and down between audience participants, for example – creates a psychological high that provides a temporary sense of success, irrespective of the long-term outcome for the viewer. The impossible dream is always just one show away for those who are so enthralled that they are critically asleep. Guru and devotee become caught up in dependence upon each other to obtain a satisfactory sense of personal existence and worth.

Globalisation, driven primarily by the economic grunt of the USA, has meant that there are many hours of television viewing time that provide little else but input from American personalities such as Oprah Winfrey, Dr Phil and Jerry Springer. The word of some of these TV gurus is almost unassailable in some social circles here in Australia.

Even to question the motivation, expertise or validity of these media-created gurus is to create hostility and spoil the coffee morning. I have noted that more explosive emotion results from a critical comment about Oprah or Dr Phil than discussions of relationships, political conflicts, poverty or global warming. Yet many of the views impressed upon us by these influential people will doubtless receive trenchant criticism in decades to come.

In global terms, the numbers of people who watch TV shows of this genre and buy the endless flow of related books and DVDs is staggering. If their message was worthwhile, we could expect their expanded influence to be producing a massive increase in wellbeing. Yet there is no substantial evidence that we have become happier or more emotionally healthy societies. What has emerged, however, is a new, very lucrative industry for the presenters and authors. There are people who, having avidly watched the shows and read the books, move on from one guru to another and pay a hefty price for the exercise through subscribing to ancillary products. However, most are little changed by this process apart from exhibiting a disturbing obsession with the latest expert.

I do not deny that real help and genuine advice worthy of broadcasting is provided sporadically by at least some of these gurus. Good may be achieved if people are inspired to go beyond mediocrity and achieve the very best that is possible realistically in their life situation. I confess that I found myself saying 'That's right!' to some snippets of advice I have heard on the *Dr. Phil* show while researching for this book. However, because pop-culture media presentations are a pastiche of sound bites with little opportunity to develop a coherent, substantial argument, it is extremely difficult to separate any apparently smart advice from dubious underlying concepts. Heresy is rarely pure untruth, but rather the absence of other balancing truths or the misrepresentation of a truth by placing it in the wrong context.

As a young jackeroo in the Australian outback in the 1950s, I learnt that to bait dingoes you do not use rubbish meat. You use an attractive bait and lace it with strychnine. The problem is that while much of the material from self-esteem gurus may be good meat, it is laced, albeit unintentionally, with psychological, social and spiritual strychnine – the underlying radical selfishness and self-obsession that characterise the myth of self-esteem. Oprah Winfrey and Dr Phil have been particularly effective in promoting aspects of this myth across the entire English-speaking and European world, and are now reaching beyond this sphere into the economically developing world.

Oprah

Oprah Winfrey started her broadcasting career in the USA in Nashville and Baltimore. In 1984 she relocated to Chicago to host WLS-TV's morning talk show *AM Chicago*, which was renamed *The Oprah Winfrey Show* a year later. Following its syndication in 1986, the show quickly became the highest-rating talk show in television history. By 2011 it was reaching more than 40 million viewers a week in the USA alone, and was licensed to 150 countries internationally.

Oprah was listed by *Time* magazine among its '100 Most Influential People in the World' from 2004–2011.[2] In 2013 she topped *Forbes* magazine's list of the world's most powerful celebrities. Although the last Oprah Winfrey Show was broadcast on 25 May 2011, its influence, and Oprah's personal influence, show no signs of abating.

In 1990, just as the notion of building self-esteem as a panacea for society's ills was emerging as a public issue, Oprah gave it an enormous boost by endorsing it, as described in the following report:

> Schools may teach it, politicians praise it, but when Oprah Winfrey does a prime-time special on it, a trend has arrived. So when the talk-show host turns her attention to the self-esteem movement in a syndicated program, the burgeoning field – blasted as a new age excuse for navel gazing – just might get some respect … she believes self-esteem will be 'one of the catch-all phrases for the '90s'.[3]

Reportedly, she once described lack of self-esteem as 'the root of all the problems in the world'.[4]

One particular issue of *O: The Oprah Magazine* provided a series of maxims from various sources, including Oprah herself. They were attractively printed on cards for readers to remove, to be used as constant reminders of these seemingly immutable 'truths'. Here is a small sample:

> I could be whatever I wanted to be, if I trusted that music, that song, that vibration of God that was inside of me. *Shirley MacLaine*
>
> Trust yourself, think for yourself, act for yourself, speak for yourself, be yourself. Imitation is suicide. *Marva Collins*
>
> Whatever your goal, you can get there if you're willing to work … The biggest adventure you can ever take is to live the life of your dreams. *Oprah*

These, and many other dictums issued by Oprah, are steeped in the myth of self-esteem.[5] 'You can be whatever you want to be' is a favourite theme, no doubt inspired by her own remarkable emergence from a troubled adolescence and sexual abuse in a small farming community to international fame and billionaire status.

The 'all about me' theme is another that comes through strongly. Incongruously, Oprah also acknowledges the importance of good relationships and consideration for others. She quotes Martin Luther King Jr's inspirational words, 'Everyone has the power for greatness – not for fame but greatness, because greatness is determined by service.'[6] On the other hand, she is also reported as saying, 'Surround yourself only with people who are going to lift you higher.'[7] How can you serve the needy and at the same time keep your distance from them?

To her credit, Oprah has often used her show to draw attention to problems in ways that are in the public interest. For example, soon after an episode of *The Oprah Winfrey Show* about child abuse, in which she urged young victims to seek adult help, a 9-year-old girl found the courage to speak to her teacher and was rescued from years of abuse.[8] Oprah also uses her immense wealth to support worthy causes. In fact, in 2005, *Business Week* named her the greatest black philanthropist in American history.

While acknowledging the good Oprah has achieved through public education and philanthropy, it is important to note that the potential to do great damage is also inherent in her position of influence. Her lack of discernment in publicising a strange assortment of products, books and ideas without regard to the validity of their proponents' claims, or indeed the welfare of her vast audience, seems quite irresponsible. She has turned many a dubious spruiker into an overnight celebrity just by virtue of the fact that they are on her show. Her penchant for presenting health-related pseudoscience as if it is fact has been condemned roundly and deservedly.[9]

High-sounding, but often vacuous, quotations or assertions are one of the hallmarks of the myth of self-esteem. These are often affirmations of love or praise for yourself. Oprah seems especially partial to this approach. I remember watching one of her shows in which she encouraged her audience to look in the mirror and say nice things to the image facing them. She said the image would then say nice things back to them. This was supposed to build their sense of self-esteem. I tried it. I told my image, 'You are a handsome, attractive young man', but the image replied, 'You've got to be joking.' If the projected image of self is untrue, then the self-esteem derived from it will also be phoney and, at some stage, reality will kick in.

I believe that Oprah has sought to distance herself from the self-esteem movement in recent years, perhaps because it has become the object of increasing criticism. However, there is no indication that she has moved away from her representations of the self as the ultimate reference point for achieving what she refers to as your 'best life'. According to a recent article in *Fortune* magazine, Oprah admits that the principle of making a difference to just one person at a time is not enough for her.[10] Her self-confessed goal (or maybe her need) is to influence millions. In 2011 she launched her own cable TV network (OWN) in the hope that this would expand her reach. It is now available in 85 million homes.

Dr Phil

Phillip McGraw, who got his start on *The Oprah Winfrey Show*, now hosts his own TV talk show called *Dr. Phil* – a syndicated, daily, one-hour show. Since its launch in 2002, it has become the second-highest-rating daytime talk show in the USA, watched by millions throughout the world. Dr Phil's stated aim is an admirable one: to help guests 'solve their problems by stripping away their emotional clutter and providing them with the tools they need to move ahead confidently in their lives'.

With the combination of his title (doctor), his field of expertise (psychology), his media personality status and his charisma, Dr Phil has a great deal of power to impact the culture. His doctorate is legitimate, but the widespread perception that Dr Phil is a practicing psychologist rests on shakier ground. Deciding he was unsuited to the clinical psychologist's role, he ceased private practice about 20 years ago and chose to retire his license in 2006. To avoid legal difficulties, he must convince TV regulators that his show is entertainment rather than psychology.[11]

Dr Phil knows how to exploit his credentials to the maximum, managing to achieve an air of authority that befits a guru's status. Each show follows a similar formula, in which Dr Phil's role is to offer his learned pronouncements, while the role of his guests is to believe him unquestioningly and make sure the audience is aware of this before the closing credits roll.

Dr Phil is the author of six books that have topped *The New York Times*' bestseller lists. Is this evidence that what he has to say is of considerable social value? Not necessarily. As long as a book is readable and engaging, it can achieve bestseller status just because it is marketed effectively. It can have a major cultural impact without any real examination of the validity of its content. For Dr Phil, his relationship with Oprah Winfrey not only launched his career in television but also virtually guaranteed him his place in *The New York Times*' bestseller lists. It was Oprah who gave him a regular segment on her show, interviewed him about his books and recommended them to her vast audiences.

This is not meant to deny Dr Phil's skills as an astute writer, or suggest that he has nothing worthwhile to say. My wife and I have discussed some of his wise advice for our own relational needs. But while Dr Phil grows rich from his bestselling book *Self Matters*, does he really deal with what matters most?[12] Although Dr Phil does offer genuine advice about improving relationships, preventing crime, and ending substance abuse, it is rooted in the promotion of individual fulfilment – the all-about-me myth – rather than the ideal of building ethical community. For example, here is a snippet from *Self Matters*:

write in as much detail as possible that life script which you would write for yourself given an unfettered choice. Do not try to please anyone or even to think about whether it is appropriate or not.

I searched the book for statements that would balance this self-focused directive by drawing attention to the importance of caring concern for the legitimate needs of others or the honouring of commitments and communal responsibilities. I searched in vain. One could be forgiven for thinking that a more appropriate title for this book might have been *Only Self Matters*.

Along with the all-about-me emphasis, we find more than a hint of the insidious be-whatever-you-want-to-be myth in this book. Dr Phil takes the reader on a subtle progression. He starts with the need to discover 'the truth of who you are', then moves on to a directive to envision 'the life chain that you want', as if the latter goal is achievable for everyone without limitation provided they are prepared to follow his advice. In addition, *Self Matters* offers techniques for becoming 'the person you have always wanted to be' and features the following assertion in bold type:

> FACT: Every one of us, you included, has within us everything we will ever need to be, do, and have anything and everything we will ever want and need.

Dr Phil has become very rich through his promises to transform people's lives. A central theme in *Self Matters* is the inference that by applying the techniques or 'tools' he describes, you will connect with 'your authentic self', a catchphrase he uses repeatedly. Doing this will require courage and effort, he says. You will need to get real and deal with misconceptions about yourself, both those imposed on you by others and those that have resulted from your own flawed thinking.

If his tools for achieving the latter goal work, I have no problem with that. However, he goes on to claim that this authentic self will be 'characterized by confidence, hope, optimism, joy, and purpose'.[13] He assures the reader that by connecting with this authentic self they will 'find more energy for [their] purposes and discover that the promise of joy and peace is indeed true'. What is more, he gives his readers the impression that if they faithfully 'trust' this authentic self — if they exercise 'self-trust' — they will be led automatically towards the fulfilment of their own freely imagined 'life script'.

I cannot accept this. If someone were to 'connect with their authentic self' by following Dr Phil's advice, they might find it *helpful*, but it would not make them *infallible*. It is self-delusion to believe otherwise. Common sense tells us that mature, psychologically healthy human beings do not always make perfect choices and decisions, or achieve all their unfettered imaginings as Dr Phil implies. Having worked for a lifetime with emotionally and mentally disturbed people, who may or may not exhibit obvious symptoms, I see it as not only ill-advised, but also dangerous, to offer people blanket encouragement to trust themselves as infallible guides. What if their judgement is clouded, or their grasp of reality impaired?

Dr Phil, like many corporate motivational gurus, often invokes religious moral language to support his statements. For example, he quotes the Bible to support his claim that only by focusing on themselves will his audience become fulfilled individuals who have the assets to spare for those who are in need.[14] He implies that Jesus himself was teaching this when he said, 'Love your neighbour as yourself'. This is a flawed interpretation, completely inconsistent with all we know about the character of Jesus. Initially embraced by much of the neo-Pentecostal church and subsequently adopted by many mainstream churches, this new religion of the self, in which you must love yourself before you can love others, has become a mantra in secular society as well. 'Charity begins at home', we hear. But for many people, charity never leaves home.

As I see it, by justifying self-centredness on apparently sound moral grounds, Dr Phil achieves the ultimate in snake-oil salesmanship: he makes the self-interested *good life* appear synonymous with the *virtuous life*. In doing so, he also subtly redefines quasi-religious terms, such as 'forgiveness', 'beliefs' and 'spiritual fulfilment', in ways that make them seem more compatible with self-interest.

For example, this is how the virtue of forgiveness is given an all-about-me twist. In *Self Matters*, as far as I have been able to determine, Dr Phil offers only one reason for working at forgiving someone who has wronged you.[15] He believes that this unresolved outside influence obscures the magnificence and the limitless possibilities of your authentic self. You therefore need to be set free so you can continue on the path to fulfilling your 'life script'. Once you are again 'congruent' with your authentic self, you may simply move on. The social damage of refusing to forgive does not come into the picture. Nor is consideration given to what is happening for the other person involved, or even the possibility of restoration of relationship through long-term efforts.[16]

If the absoluteness, the overwhelming self-confidence, and the unqualified guarantees of presenters like Dr Phil were mouthed by religious preachers, they would be despised by popular culture. Apparently, no such ethical demands are made of the high priests of self-esteem. While their language may be pastoral, even religious, and reassuringly concerned for the welfare of their audience or interviewees, all too often their messages are tainted by the fact that positive market outcomes have become a major driving force for their activities.

Self-help gurus

Bookshelves of commercial outlets these days offer an abundance of so-called self-help books addressing a wide variety of topics. Many of these promote some aspect of the myth of self-esteem. A great deal of self-help information is also disseminated through unregulated pop-culture journalism, particularly in magazines that target women. The democratisation of the arts and current affairs, alongside the ubiquitous power of the electronic media, has created an unregulated context for self-referenced gurus to become experts overnight. Virtually anyone can be an expert. What once would have been viewed as the lunatic fringe has now become mainstream.

Some years ago while in France, I saw an interviewer on European BBC TV seriously introduce the world's expert on angels, who then proceeded to draw on this supposed expertise to advocate a wide range of self-help 'psychological' therapies. Genuine experts in the counselling and therapy fields are expressing serious concern about self-diagnosis, self-medication and therapy by television, seeing it as a potentially dangerous development of recent times.

Steve Salerno, an American business writer and investigative journalist, has expressed his concerns about the self-help movement in a controversial book entitled *SHAM: How the Gurus of the Self-Help Movement Make Us Helpless.*[17] He reports that the market for the 'self-improvement' industry – just one aspect of what he calls the Self-Help and Actualisation Movement (SHAM) – was expected to approach 12 billion dollars per annum in the USA by 2008. He writes convincingly about the ethically questionable commercial practices of some of the gurus of this movement, including deliberate strategies for drumming up repeat business to keep profits flowing.

In his zeal to condemn, Salerno at times adopts such a shot-gun approach that he peppers the innocent as well as the guilty, the helpful as well as the unhelpful, with his barrages. Nonetheless, I see merit in this book if it serves as a wake-up call to readers who are being hoodwinked by unscrupulous 'gurus of the self-help movement' described by Salerno.

An extremely diverse assortment of activities and products are now amalgamated under the 'self-help' banner, and this is a source of confusion for many people. Strictly speaking, most of the products and programs currently being touted in this way are representative of the self-improvement industry, rather than the self-help movement.

Few recognise that the original self-help movement began with the formation of support groups such as Alcoholics Anonymous, which now include related groups for gamblers and addicts. In this context, the term '*self*-help' is something of a misnomer, because the emphasis in such groups is not on the isolated individual. Rather, participants become part of a mutually supportive network, and are called upon to help each other through mutual sharing of their experiences. They are also encouraged to reach beyond themselves to a 'higher power' for help to address their problem. I want to affirm some of the excellent work being done by such groups, which were established, and still run, on a not-for-profit basis. In stark contrast, present day commercially driven 'self-help' gurus have moved far from the guiding principles of such groups, and are deserving of Salerno's scathing criticism.

Michael Lallo, in his article about 'the seven biggest self-help myths', acknowledges that some self-help books are written by qualified professionals and contain sensible advice based on research and fact. He admits that even some of the dodgier titles may contain 'nuggets of wisdom among the mountains of claptrap'.[18] Generally, however, he condemns them as riddled with clichés and advice that simply does not work. I agree with this assessment. Nevertheless, millions of people buy these books and swear by them. As a result, self-help is a growth industry that can boast a remarkable crop of overnight millionaires among its motivational authors and presenters.

Religious gurus

It is not only the individual who is at risk because of the self-esteem myth and its focus on self-interest. Precariously balanced institutions such as religion, education and psychology have all been deeply affected. Here, I highlight one aspect of this: the emergence of dynamic religious leaders who are preaching the myth of self-esteem.

For some decades, the great religions of the world have been incorporating alien beliefs of a culture of self-gratification and greed with seemingly little resistance. It has become common to find established religions being misrepresented as soothing analgesics, available to remove the symptoms of self-centeredness, yet without challenging the root causes of greed-based stress.

A 'sexier', made-over version of God is touted by pop-Christianity, TV God channels and Christian self-esteem gurus, each of which promise a liberating, less repressive faith. Robert Schuller was an early and influential proponent of such seductive theology. For many years he preached every Sunday from the pulpit of the Crystal Cathedral on his TV show, *Hour of Power*, which was the world's most widely watched church service. I regard many of his books and presentations as laced with the myth of self-esteem, including his book entitled *Self-Esteem, The New Reformation* published in 1982.[19]

Some Christian TV evangelists now sound little different from any other self-esteem-focused motivator, except for an occasional mention of Jesus. The rush to materialism and the self-focus embraced by these new Christian gurus, ostentatiously dressed in a new designer suit for every telecast, is bizarre. How did the television evangelists and the new mega-churches come to embrace a materialistic self-esteem theology so alien to the teachings of the one after whom the Christian church is named? Even those only moderately familiar with Jesus will know that this is not consistent with his teachings and lifestyle. I see this trend as a damaging deviation from the inclusiveness and liberation expounded not only by Jesus Christ, but also by the founders of other great world religions.

Buddhism has become equally corrupted. In today's context of individualism and self-advancement, the techniques of the Buddha, rather than the meanings of his teaching, are offered to jaded materialists by corporate motivators. Mantra and meditation are used to overcome the stress of financial go-getting, as a means of enhancing the individual's self-centred quest for success. Having studied Buddhism as part of my doctoral coursework, I am astonished at the incongruity of this. In its essence, Buddhism is about self-denial and self-transcendence. Just as jarring to me are images of Buddhist monks being used in advertisements for the consumptive and materialistic lifestyle. The Buddha would be appalled. This is such a distortion of his message of detachment from the corrosive effects of materialistic desire and aggression.

In the nineteenth century, America specialised in religious charlatans and 'snake-oil' salesmen, who offered miraculous cures through their expensive but ineffective potions. Australia had its equivalent, the goanna-oil salesmen, who guaranteed that their product was so penetrating it would soak through the glass container to the label on the bottle. While today we mock the religious and market manipulators of yesteryear, some religious gurus exercise the same deceptive and manipulative role in the twenty-first century.

The infamous German priest Johann Tetzel was an unscrupulous salesman of the early sixteenth century, who sold 'indulgences' to parishioners who were seeking to ease their loved one's passage in the afterlife. His marketing slogan translates as 'When the coin in the coffer rings, the soul from purgatory springs'.[20] There are today some preachers in the Western world who, Tetzel-like, beguile an impressionable and anxious public to give money generously (to themselves or a nominated cause) in order to receive the 'abundant' life promised by Jesus, here and hereafter.[21] I recall one popular TV evangelist who declared that, when you give to God, you receive a 'receipt' from him, which you can 'cash in' later on demand when you have a need for prosperity or health.

While hopefully in most cases a fair portion of the funds acquired by this type of religious coercion are directed towards worthy causes, such giving may also serve to ensure that the preachers themselves receive abundantly and live sumptuously.[22] Time and again, I have heard religious gurus telling us not to hang out with negative thinkers and losers if we want the very best of the good things that God wants for us. This is a far cry from the tradition of Jesus, who consistently associated with the marginalised losers of his society – the physical, spiritual and social outcasts.

The emphasis on individual acquisition of wealth and possessions is also completely out of touch with Jesus' view of the abundant life. Once, on the world's largest Christian network, I saw a hyper-emotional, screaming woman preacher assert: 'God says you can have your own house in the next thirty days. What you have in your heart is greater than what you have in your pocket – your faith.'[23] A preacher in another program assured his audience that by faith they could have anything they wanted in just two weeks.

Those who control the dissemination of this new, secular gospel have the money to drive the multi-media machine. Largely, the money is raised from fees charged for public presentations, mass marketing of videos and DVDs and writing bestsellers that tell of their success. Highly questionable inducements may be used to manipulate the public to give. Some religious gurus have become financial high flyers through using their skills to promote industries that sail close to the edge of illegal pyramid selling. Dodgy religious practitioners of this ilk often find a loophole to escape legal action not available to their secular counterparts.

As is typical of gurus of the myth of self-esteem in general, the sales pitch of religious gurus places the onus for success on the individual under their influence. When seekers fail to obtain the promised miracle – despite having carefully followed all instructions, submitted to recommended rituals and believed with all their heart – they are left to face the blame themselves for their lack of faith or failure of character. This can keep them returning again and again at great personal cost.

The line between moral–religious values and economic greed has become thoroughly blurred in the ethos and presentations of religious gurus. Most of them initially learnt the art of passionate public discourse through spiritually driven presentations of Christian virtues and religious conversion. Some who began by telling how religious surrender changed their life and transformed their social relationships now make presentations about how to get rich and assert your own authority over every aspect of life.

Religious gurus have jumped on the self-esteem bandwagon with a spiritualised version of its mythology. They preach the be-whatever-you-want-to-be myth – whatever you desire can be yours and you can have it now – with no thought of delaying gratification in deference to a higher cause or power. They preach and embody a gospel that is all about me.

Gurus who target the young

Many youth-oriented lecturers, psychologists, educators and other experts have bought into the self-esteem movement. I have discovered extremely well-illustrated and well-written books for primary school and even preschool children aggressively pushing this cause. Diana Looman's storybook *The Lovables in the Kingdom of Self-Esteem* is an example of this.[24] Her young readers are told that chanting a feel-good formula – *I am lovable! I am lovable! I am lovable!* – is the key to transporting themselves into a mystical, idyllically happy Kingdom of Self-Esteem. In this way, at a tender age, our children are subtly introduced to the myth that boosting their self-esteem by intoning a one-size-fits-all 'positive' mantra is the way to achieve happiness.

In this book, a long list of affirmations then follows, each presented by an appealing animal character who claims to exhibit a 'lovable' quality: I am courageous, capable, gentle and strong, kind, special, unique, beautiful, positive, polite, full of joy and thankful, co-operative, calm and relaxed, peaceful inside. I respect and trust myself, I like to learn, do my best, share with others, have fun, and so on.

It is true that some of these qualities may be intrinsic and the child may simply need to be encouraged to recognise them. However, others have to be earned and may, or may not, develop over time depending on to the individual's circumstances and genetic makeup. Make-believe is not going to engender qualities that the child lacks. Nor is it the way to idyllic happiness. I believe it is more likely to promote feelings of rejection, guilt, inadequacy, anger or hopelessness in the child who recognises that they fall short of these ideals in one or more respects.[25] They may even end up regarding themselves as *un*lovable.

A regional high school invited our Values4Life team to be part of a full day's program at which their senior high students would consider identity, values, relationships and civic responsibility. Several groups had been invited to present to these teens and there was no commonality of worldview. We were last on the program but we arrived early enough to assess other presentations.

The presentation immediately before ours was on the subject of self-esteem. The vivacious, competent female presenter was teaching that the degree to which you were willing to make eye contact with another person was an indication of the level of your self-esteem. The idea was that people who do not look confidently into other people's eyes lack self-esteem. Her interactive exercises involved young people pairing off and staring into one another's eyes. This, she asserted, would help reinforce their sense of self and confidence.

My instant response to this manipulative presentation was a mixture of mild anger, concern for the students, and academic conflict with the presenter's viewpoint. This arose not only from my very different view of the needs of young people – from marginalised and homeless street kids to wealthy private high school students – gained through some 40 years of involvement with them, but also from my background in cultural anthropology. A significant proportion of people in diverse cultures would find the woman's presentation quite offensive. The fact that you do not meet the eyes of another may have little to do with self-esteem. In many cultures, you may only stare into the eyes of another on the basis of relationship or implied invitation. Such eye contact may even be regarded as an unthinkable intrusion or an act of aggression.[26]

In high schools, a variety of presenters are promoting self-esteem mythology through popular classes or seminars of uncertain quality. This includes footballers, whose experience is very unlikely to have equipped them to be the psychological role models for young adolescents.

Unfortunately, young people often adopt dysfunctional cultural icons as their role models, especially popular, highly successful performers in sport or the music industry. After all, they appear to have all the accoutrements of the good life and high self-esteem: individual freedom, wealth, peer admiration and social status. Many of these celebrities make use of their stories of humble origins, deprived childhoods and struggles to overcome obstacles. Indeed, as Mackay says, 'it's positively modish to brag about the mountains you've had to climb to get to the top'.[27] This encourages young fans to believe that they too can be whatever they want to be, thereby reinforcing this myth – yet the celebrity's sense of self-esteem may have been irrelevant to their rise to fame. It is more likely to have come about by determined effort in the midst of negative circumstances, rather than a focus on feeling good about themselves.

Sadly, all too often the lives of our young people's idols exemplify social and ethical failure. Eventually, too late to stem the damage, the now-aging pop icons may publish tell-all stories, in which they admit that their lifestyle and messages to young people in the past were a disaster. Now detoxed and with a money-making story to tell, they are simply moving on. Unfortunately, this can give young people the impression that it is possible by sheer will power to recover from drug or alcohol addiction and make a fantastic life for yourself. What they do not tell is the financial price they have paid along the way – for the best clinics, the best psychologists, the best personal trainers – a price that is far beyond the reach of their adoring fans. They may also underplay the devastating emotional costs of their journey.

Gurus: help or harm?

As can be seen from this chapter, I am deeply concerned about the influence wielded by unregulated, market-driven, often untrained gurus who are promulgating the myth of self-esteem.

I acknowledge that an element of confrontational reality therapy on an entertainment-oriented TV show – if combined with professional follow up, as provided by some presenters – may be of value to the people who participate. Helping people confront their failures and hurts, both ethical and relational, may become the doorway to change. However, many professional therapists in private practice must be aghast at the public coercion and the lack of respect for the individuals' privacy and confidentiality that are intrinsic to such TV shows, in which participants are encouraged to reveal intimate details of their problems. I find this kind of exploitation of human misery – for the financial gain and enhanced status of the presenter and the voyeuristic entertainment of the audience – decidedly tacky.

Western societies are not becoming emotionally healthier and happier, despite the concerted efforts of these gurus of the myth of self-esteem. My contention is that their focus on self as a basis for improvement of the emotional health and wellbeing of an individual (or a society) is self-defeating: ironically, some of the symptoms that various forms of media-based therapy purport to alleviate may actually result from the very worldview they promote. We need seriously to consider the possibility that such gurus may be diminishing, rather than boosting, our sense of wellbeing and self-worth – and contributing to misery rather than increasing happiness.

8
A Rising Tide of Dissent

I became aware years ago that I was not the only person who had serious reservations about the self-esteem movement and related myths. Signs of disillusionment began appearing in the media: I saw an article entitled 'It's not about me' in a UK newspaper; I watched an interview on *Larry King Live* with a corporate motivator, whose new book was entitled *The Power of We*. Since then, I have noted a rising tide of dissent, merging with and reinforcing concerns I have been expressing for many years. Increasing numbers of people are discovering that the myth of self-esteem is not working for individuals or our societies.

Alarm bells

Weaknesses in claims about self-esteem have been evident for a long time. In California in the late 1980s, the state governor set up a special taskforce to examine politician John Vasconcellos's claim that boosting young people's self-esteem would prevent a range of societal problems (see chapter 1). One of its briefs was to review the relevant literature and assess whether there was support for this new approach. An author of the resulting report wrote in the introduction that 'one of the disappointing aspects of every chapter in this volume ... is how low the associations between self-esteem and its [presumed] consequences are in research to date.'[1] Unfortunately, this early expression of concern was largely ignored.

Carol Craig reviews more recent warnings about the self-esteem movement in an online article 'A short history of self-esteem', citing the research of five professors of psychology. Craig's article and related documents are worth reading if you are interested in exploring this issue in depth.[2] The following is my summary of her key conclusions about self-esteem:

- There is no evidence that self-image enhancing techniques, aimed at boosting self-esteem directly, foster improvements in objectively measured 'performance'.
- Many people who consider themselves to have high self-esteem tend to grossly overestimate their own abilities, as assessed by objective tests of their performance, and may be insulted and threatened whenever anyone asserts otherwise.
- Low self-esteem is not a risk factor for educational problems, or problems such as violence, bullying, delinquency, racism, drug-taking or alcohol abuse.
- Obsession with self-esteem has contributed to an 'epidemic of depression' and is undermining the life skills and resilience of young people.
- Attempts to boost self-esteem are encouraging narcissism and a sense of entitlement.
- The pursuit of self-esteem has considerable costs and may undermine the wellbeing of both individuals and societies.

Some of these findings were brought to wider public attention in an article entitled 'The trouble with self-esteem', written by psychologist Lauren Slater, which appeared in *The New York Times* in 2002.[3] Related articles, far too many to mention individually in this book, have emerged, alongside many books in which authors express their concerns about various aspects of the myth of self-esteem.[4] There is particular concern about what we are doing to our children.

Self-esteem myths and our children

The following comments from eminent child psychologist and author Robert Coles, published in 1976, now seem even more apt:

> There's nothing so depressing as being locked up in oneself. There's nothing as liberating as finding a way to work with others on real problems that require energy and commitment. The other direction is one of apathetic self-regard – a malignant process and the prelude to depression. Which is the direction, God save us, some educators, psychiatrists and parents have too often pointed our children.[5]

Self-esteem mythology has become deeply embedded in approaches to education and parenting in Western countries, often in ways that are not instantly recognisable. In response, many reputable psychologists, social analysts and youth specialists are now speaking out about the potential dangers of aspects of existing approaches, and are seeing the need for humans to rise above self, even in childhood.

Inappropriate application of self-esteem-focused strategies to education, and subsequently to parenting, can be traced back to the late 1980s, when the notion of boosting self-esteem was adopted as a primary educational goal. Since that time, wherever this idea has taken hold throughout the world, myriad techniques have been introduced in attempts to achieve this goal. Some of these may be harmless or even useful, but many are ludicrous and some have the potential to harm the emotional development of our children. Such techniques, which I expect will be familiar to parents and teachers alike, include:

- teachers who are encouraged to praise continuously, regardless of actual accomplishment, and use class material that

contains affirmations of the you-are-special, you-are-important, you-are-beautiful variety
- preference for educational books and children's literature that is designed to achieve the same purpose
- the widespread practice of grade inflation, in which everyone is marked 'above average', never 'unsatisfactory', and no one is given 'excellent' in case this damages the self-esteem of those who receive a lesser grading
- an avoidance of testing children's skills altogether, so no one can feel bad about their poor results
- the lavish distribution of certificates, ribbons and awards, supposedly to affirm each child's sense of being 'special' – simply turning up at a sports carnival or award ceremony may be sufficient to warrant a special award.

Many parents, caught up in this societal trend, are reinforcing such practices in their dealings with their children, seemingly afraid to correct or disagree with them for fear of causing damage to their fragile 'self-esteem'.

The downside of over-praising children

A well-researched book entitled *NurtureShock: New Thinking about Children* includes extreme examples of ludicrous self-esteem-focused strategies.[6] For example, there are schools where children skip (or jump rope) without ropes to avoid tripping. There are soccer games played without counting goals so no one has to face the ignominy of scoring the least (or being on the losing team) and everyone gets a trophy. The authors believe that overpraised children are ill-equipped to deal with failure, and suggest that this encourages cheating. Consistent with this is a report of a survey of more than 12,000 high school students in the USA in 2002, which concluded that 'cheating, stealing and lying by high school students have continued their alarming, decade-long upward spiral'.[7]

NurtureShock also describes a study by Carol Dweck of Columbia University, which provides evidence that giving our children unwarranted 'ego-boosting' praise may backfire. Four hundred fifth-graders were given a fairly easy puzzle to do and told their score. Half were praised for being smart; the rest were praised for working hard to achieve a good result. They were then given the choice of an easier or a harder puzzle. Most of those praised for being smart chose the easier puzzle (thus ensuring further praise for their smartness) while 90% of those praised for effort chose the harder task.

Child psychologist John Irvine is another who has spoken out against educators and experts who claim that children need constant praise to ensure high self-esteem.[8] Irvine offers 'praise junkie' parents the following advice:

- Praising children for something over which they have no control, such as intelligence, makes them fearful of doing anything that might tarnish that image.
- Encouraging children's effort, over which they do have control, is likely to result in more effort the next time.
- When rewarding children for something, encourage or praise the effort or the action rather than the ego. For example, say 'I love the way you try so hard' rather than 'you must be the cleverest kid in the class'.
- Use intermittent reinforcement, rather than continual praise and reward, otherwise a child will stop as soon as the praise stops.

I firmly believe in nurturing children lovingly by providing appropriate praise and encouragement, but problems arise when unconditional love is interpreted as unconditional praise. Roy Baumeister, aware of the potential for indiscriminate praise to pave the way for narcissism, recommends using praise 'only as a reward for socially desirable behavior and self-improvement'.[9]

There is genuine concern that narcissism is on the increase

among young people, if not in its more pathological forms then at least as a general disposition. As a clinical condition, narcissistic personality disorder is characterised by: a grandiose sense of self-importance; a sense of being special and entitlement to special recognition, treatment and privileges; arrogance; a need for excessive admiration and envy; a preoccupation with fantasies of unlimited success, brilliance and beauty; exploitative relationships; a lack of empathy and an inability to recognise the needs of others; and reacting to criticism with feelings of rage, shame or humiliation (which may or may not be expressed).[10] There are disturbingly familiar echoes of self-esteem myths in this — *it's all about me, I can be whatever I want to be, I need to feel good and look good, it's never my fault.*

Jeanette Twenge and her colleagues drew together the results of studies involving large numbers of college students throughout the USA, all of whom were posed the same series of forty 'Narcissistic Personality Inventory' questions.[11] They found an alarming increase in narcissism between the early 1980s and 2009, a period over which boosting self-esteem became a major focus of the education system. While this in itself does not prove that the self-esteem movement has caused the increase in narcissism, Twenge and others are now suggesting that such a link may exist.[12]

Some of the students who participated in the narcissism studies were also asked questions about work attitudes.[13] Unlike students who were entering the work force in 1976 or 1991, those entering in 2006 (dubbed GenMe) placed a premium on rewards such as higher salaries and status but also wanted more leisure time. She saw the disconnection between their expectations and reality and their unhealthy sense of entitlement as entirely consistent with the overall shift towards narcissism she had observed over time.

Psychologists Laura Smith and Charles Elliott in their book *Hollow Kids* also argue strongly that overinflated 'self-esteem' may inflict damage on our children.[14] As well as narcissism with its increased risk of aggression and violence, this may include a distorted body image related to tattooing, body piercing, anorexia and bulimia. Other possible outcomes are a ceaseless quest to feel good, which may manifest as insatiable materialism, shoplifting and substance abuse.

Young people who have grown up through the self-esteem-boosting era are themselves becoming aware that all is not well. One has described the way she, as an adult, now feels they were 'screwed over' by parenting that gave them such an inflated sense of themselves that regular, ordinary life seems like an underachievement:

> Our parents told us we were special and that we could do or be anything we wanted when we grew up ... We're nothing. We're useless. But surely this is inevitable; after all. Of the hundreds and thousands of people classified as generation Y not all of us can be brilliant, can we? Not all of us can have been as special and smart as our parents led us to believe ... So why did they lead us to believe that we were? Perhaps they did it to make themselves look good as parents.[15]

I have the feeling that sometimes our approach to parenting is really about our own struggles – our own search for self-esteem and significance through our children – in areas where we feel we have failed in the past. Or perhaps, at the other extreme, we may be compensating for our own experience of parents who were unable to express their feelings for us and felt it was their duty to keep us humble. Whatever our motivations may be – and they may well arise from an intense desire to love and care – there is growing evidence that excessive, indiscriminate praise carries serious negative consequences.

Educators speak out

> *A TV documentary presented some years ago showed a kindergarten class being given the following exercise, presumably aimed at boosting their self-esteem. The teacher had made an attractively decorated 'magic box' with a small curtain that could be pulled aside. Having delivered a preamble*

designed to engender a sense of mystery and high expectation in the children, she invited each one to come forward in turn and look into the magic box where they would see 'the most important person in the world'. Inside the box was a mirror! She was teaching tiny children to have grandiose, unrealistic opinions of themselves and their specialness – and potentially sowing the seeds of narcissism.

Nina Shokraii, an influential US education analyst and commentator, believes it is 'crucial to delegitimize the education establishment's mindless glorification of self-esteem'.[16] She sees little reason to believe that self-esteem is pivotal to academic achievement, or even necessary for academic success. Her particular concern is the welfare of children from low socio-economic groups, many of whom are black, because it is generally assumed that they have low self-esteem that must be corrected. She says schools are cheating these children 'into settling for inflated egos instead of increased knowledge'.

Shokraii describes a study in the early 1990s in which the academic skills of elementary school students in Japan, Taiwan, China and the USA were compared. The American students received relatively low academic rankings but scored higher than the Asian students when asked to assess their own skills in the subjects tested. In other words, they felt good about their relatively poor performance. Possible explanations offered by the psychologists involved, Harold Stevenson and James Stigler, were that the focus of the teachers in the USA was much more on 'sensitivity to students' egos' whereas the Asian teachers' focus was on clarity in their teaching. Also 'American teachers avoid criticizing poor performance, fearing damage to students' self-esteem', whereas Asian teachers tend to 'regard mistakes as an index of what remains to be learned through persistence and increased effort'.

Recently the headmaster of a prestigious private college in Sydney expressed his disillusionment with the 'concept of self-esteem'. He was reported as saying:

In some ways it has been the most damaging educational concept that has ever been conceived. We couldn't do anything that would upset or harm the self-esteem of students, which was very fragile we were led to believe ... That is when we stopped our proper work in the character formation in young people. If we are serious about building resilience, we have to let them fail.'[17]

In his view failure encourages children to think creatively, whereas fear of making a mistake inhibits participation. The President of the NSW Secondary Principals Council followed this with a call for the abandonment of 'false praise'.

I sympathise with a British teacher who in 2009 saw the educational system as one in which trying to get students to feel good took priority over education and that 'low self-esteem' had become a cop-out for poor behaviour.[18] Once the diagnosis or assumption of low self-esteem has been applied, the teacher said, attempts to raise self-esteem − through praise, special attention, and other miscellaneous treats − are usually indistinguishable from rewarding the child for their bad behaviour. Thus, teachers are expected to praise students who are least deserving of it, and face being criticised for their poor skills when the misbehaviour continues.

Some educators have been aware for many years that it is futile to encourage students to feel good about themselves without linking this with appropriate behaviour and performance or effort.[19] After reading a newspaper article on this topic, an Australian teacher responded:

> In the past I have written articles lauding the importance of self-esteem as a key ingredient in the educational process ... I had become a chorister to the mantra of encouraging a healthy sense of self-esteem in young people. Hugh Mackay's commentary yesterday has arrested decades of thinking − maybe what I should have been promoting all this time is not a healthy sense of self-esteem but a healthy sense of self-respect?[20]

Nevertheless, unhelpful practices continue in our schools to the detriment of our children.

Making sense of it all

Some people in conversation with me on the topic of self-esteem have argued that my concerns all come down to semantics: to my interpretation of the term 'self-esteem'. Of course, interpretation is very subjective, and I agree that in one word there may be a whole world of connected ideas. I do not, for example, have the same reaction to 'self-worth', 'self-respect' or 'identity' as I do now towards the term 'self-esteem'. The latter term has, I believe, developed a subtle but distinct connotation that goes beyond the simple understanding that I, as a unique individual, have an intrinsic value. Some dictionaries now give two meanings for self-esteem: (1) self-respect, a sense of one's own worth; (2) self-conceit, an exaggerated opinion of one's own qualities or abilities.[21] The first is well established; the second, added more recently, strongly validates my uneasiness about this term.

Broadly speaking, self-esteem refers to how we feel about or how we value ourselves.[22] Nathaniel Branden, an influential figure in the development of present-day concepts of self-esteem, now offers a more complex definition: 'the experience of being competent to cope with the basic challenges of life and being worthy of happiness'.[23] According to Branden, *genuine* self-esteem needs to be based on objective standards or 'pillars'. For an adult, these include self-acceptance based on realistic self-evaluation, and living responsibly and with integrity. *Pseudo*-self-esteem, in contrast, Branden says, depends solely upon external sources, such as social status, physical appearance or the admiration or approval of others. People who lack genuine self-esteem will tend to compensate by relying on external sources. However, as these cannot realistically enhance feelings of competence, such people will feel insecure and easily threatened.

For me, this distinction between genuine self-esteem and

pseudo-self-esteem makes sense of the two very different definitions of this term in dictionaries. How ironic it is that the cultural myth that has arisen out of the self-esteem movement, a movement Branden is credited with fathering, is now characterised by practices that strongly promote dependence on external factors and therefore foster what he has defined as pseudo-self-esteem.

Psychologists now recognise many categories of self-esteem, including Branden's 'genuine' and 'pseudo' self-esteem. The widely used Rosenberg Scale measures 'global self-esteem': an individual's positive or negative attitude towards themselves as a totality. However, because this method relies directly on people's opinions about themselves, it cannot distinguish between those who evaluate themselves accurately and those who do not.[24] Attempts are being made to assess implicit (intrinsic, 'unfake-able') self-esteem as distinct from explicit (subjective, self-reported) self-esteem, but this is proving problematic.[25]

Confusion is inevitable when a multifaceted term such as self-esteem is used with different meanings in different contexts, and sometimes even in the same context. Perhaps we need to revisit the notion of self-esteem and come up with definitions and distinctive terminology and methodology that will help us communicate exactly what we mean. For example, when we use the term 'self-esteem' are we referring to a 'healthy' or 'unhealthy' self-assessment or a mixture of both? Hugh Mackay highlights current confusion about terminology when he writes:

> Self-esteem is like a frothy substitute for self-respect, and we'd be doing our children a favour if we explained the difference. They need to know, as early as possible, that hard-won self-respect is a healthier and more robust emotional state than floating along in a fragile bubble of self-esteem.[26]

As I see it, if feeling good about ourselves is based on appropriate behaviour and living well in relationship with others, it is healthy. If it is artificially induced as a result of unrealistic beliefs about our abilities or an exaggerated sense of self-importance, it is not.

This is not a new idea. More than 2000 years ago in his classic work on ethics, Aristotle proposed that people who are truly happy not only like their lives but also love themselves – or, as we might say, have an appropriate sense of self-worth or self-esteem. However, for him happiness was not merely a vague feeling of wellbeing. It was grounded in virtuous activity. He carefully distinguished 'true self-love, which characterizes the virtuous person, from vulgar self-love, which characterizes morally defective types ... [who] love themselves in the sense that they love material goods and advantages. They desire to secure these things even at the expense of other people.'[27]

Generally, we would have to say that the concept of self-esteem promoted by the myth of self-esteem falls into Aristotle's category of vulgar self-love – that is, a one-dimensional dependence on personal feelings, being satisfied and fulfilled as 'me' in isolation from any responsibility to others. If Aristotle's ideas are right, that is no way to pursue happiness! In the 17th century, Milton, one of the first to mention the term self-esteem in the English language, wrote in his classic work *Paradise Lost*: 'Oft times nothing profits more, Than self-esteem, grounded on just and right.' Clearly, he also saw a strong link between self-esteem and appropriate behaviour.

William James, a major influence in the emerging science of psychology just before the turn of the nineteenth century, proposed that self-esteem depends on the ratio of two factors:[28]

$$\text{self-esteem} = \frac{\text{success}}{\text{pretensions}}$$

Here, 'success' means feeling that we are achieving aims that are important to us, while 'pretensions' means our expectations of ourselves. James is saying that self-esteem can be boosted either by increasing our success or by lowering our pretentions. If this is the case, the practice of manufacturing unrealistic, exaggerated pretensions about ourselves (a characteristic of the myth of self-esteem) is more likely to leave us feeling bad about ourselves than increase our self-esteem. James wrote: 'How pleasant is the day when we give up striving to be young – or slender! Thank God! we say, *those* illusions are gone.'

Seeking to pump up our self-esteem by inflating our pretensions as a primary intervention invokes the law of diminishing returns – the harder we try the less will be the return on our efforts. On the other hand, even if our pretensions (our expectations of ourselves) are appropriate to our situation – neither too high, nor too low – they will have no effect on our self-esteem unless we make an effort to live up to them.

Martin Seligman believes that the beauty of James's definition lies in the fact that it highlights two key components of self-esteem – feeling good and doing well.[29] He defines 'doing well' as having 'good commerce' with the world around us – that is, engaging positively with others and behaving well towards them.[30] At one end of the spectrum, he says, 'are those who advocate feeling good as the primary goal'. They believe that how we *feel* about ourselves is paramount, while how we *do* in the world is a fortunate by-product. At the other end are those like Seligman himself 'who advocate doing well in the world as the primary goal, with feeling good only a delicious by-product'.[31] For me this goes to the heart of the present confusion:

The meaning of the term 'self-esteem' has become so degraded within the myth spawned by the self-esteem movement that the connection between feeling good and doing well has all but disappeared.

The overwhelming emphasis of the myth of self-esteem is on feeling good. Doing well, let alone doing good for others, hardly seems to matter at all. Instead of concentrating on values and civil responsibility, which are important aspects of doing well, we and our children are increasingly being urged to centre our lives on ourselves, our achievements, our appearance, our competitiveness and our status in the pecking order.

Seligman (and others) are now suggesting that our starting point should not be boosting self-esteem but rather boosting performance, the 'doing well' part of James's equation. He notes that two generations ago, children's books and primers for first and second grades were about doing well and achieving good outcomes – a typical example being *The Little Engine that Could*. Now, primers are much more about feeling good and having high self-esteem than about good dealings with the world. He says, 'What needs improving in kids with low self-esteem is not directly how they feel, but the skills for good commerce with the world.'[32]

Because a self-esteem focus is inevitably inward looking, the widespread emphasis on building self-esteem flags the fact that we in the West are living in radically individualistic societies. It is therefore imperative that any attempts to boost the 'performance' aspect of self-esteem should focus on attitudes and behaviour, rather than the acquisition of stereotypical symbols of personal achievement. The best way forward is not to surround ourselves with symbols of success and voices declaring how wonderful we are. Rather, we need a changed worldview and a reason and purpose that will lift our vision beyond ourselves.

Room for optimism

Googling the name 'Seligman' retrieves an astonishingly large number of hits. These refer not only to the man himself but also to a fast-growing movement founded by him and his colleagues: the positive psychology movement.[33] Seligman's definition of positive psychology is the scientific study of the strengths and virtues that enable individuals and communities to thrive. He writes: 'Our message is to remind our field that psychology is not just the study of pathology, weakness, and damage; it is also the study of strength and virtue. Treatment is not just fixing what is broken; it is nurturing what is best.'[34]

Seligman, although acknowledged as an expert in the study of depression, has now shifted his emphasis from *what is wrong* to asking *what is right and useful?* How can we *prevent* rather than *cure* malaise? His focus is on methods for increasing optimism rather than self-esteem. The term 'positive psychology' can now be found on many websites promoting professional courses, books, programs and educational resources. However, discernment is needed. As with all popular movements, there is a real danger that over time (if it has not happened already), many self-referenced gurus and pop psychologists will jump on this bandwagon and exploit it for their own purposes, capitalising on the 'positive psychology' catchcry, but distorting the original concept in the process.

Seligman encourages the development of an optimistic outlook, a concept introduced in his book *The Optimistic Child*, first published in 1995, and subsequently developed in *Learned Optimism*. He says that if optimism is high, the individual will tend to see the world as benevolent and expect good things to happen. If pessimism predominates, however, they will see the world as malevolent and expect bad things to happen.

When I began to read *The Optimistic Child* and discovered the emergence of child optimism programs, I wondered if this was the myth of self-esteem in another guise. I am now convinced that it is not. Seligman is encouraging the mix of realism and idealism that our children need, not the unqualified fantasy that they can be and do anything without limitation. 'Optimism is a tool with a certain clear set of benefits: it fights depression, it promotes achievement and produces better health,' he says.[35] Furthermore, he is convinced that optimism is an attribute that can be learned.[36] This includes learning to expect hard experiences and occasional down periods so that dealing with problems becomes part of normal life.

Seligman advocates what he calls 'flexible optimism', which means being able to move towards either optimism or pessimism depending on the situation you are confronting and the consequences of failing.[37] If the cost of failure is small, he recommends optimism. For example, if you are anxious about getting to know a potential romantic partner or if you are a salesperson having trouble contacting a new client, you are not going to lose a great deal if it does not go well. On the other hand, if the cost of failure is potentially catastrophic, for example, if you are contemplating an affair that could end your marriage, pessimism is more appropriate. 'What we want is the ability to recognise the difference between situations that call for optimism, trying harder, and the situations that call for realism and pessimism.'[38]

Thus, despite his strong commitment to helping people become more optimistic, Seligman acknowledges that pessimists are more realistic than optimists, and better at acknowledging danger, assessing how much control they have, and remembering their successes and failures. To illustrate the need for balance between what he calls 'optimism of the will and pessimism of the intellect', he describes each of us as being like the CEO of a large company. The CEO must balance the charge-ahead mentality of the sales force (their optimism of the will) against the gloomy predictions (the pessimism of the intellect) of the accountants, both of whom are essential to a successful operation.

Healthy optimism, like healthy self-esteem, is well founded. It is based in reality, and built on a positive life characterised by good citizenship and the recognition that life does not deliver whatever you want. This is quite different from the phony, feel-good optimism of the myth of self-esteem, which is sustained largely by self-deception and wishful thinking. Barbara Ehrenreich suggests that instead of teaching our children unrealistic, feel-good 'positive thinking' we should be teaching them critical thinking.[39]

A crucial aspect of maintaining healthy optimism is learning to discern realistically what you can change and what you cannot change. A prayer adopted by the Alcoholics Anonymous organisation more than sixty years ago expresses this beautifully:

> God grant me the serenity to accept the things I cannot change,
> Courage to change the things I can,
> And wisdom to know the difference.

The principles described by Seligman are now being put into practice in an innovative school-based program, offered by his colleagues Jane Gillham and Karen Reivich from the University of Pennsylvania.[40] This program, the Penn Resiliency Program, has been implemented in various states in the USA, as well as Australia, the UK, Canada and China, and has proved remarkably effective in staving off symptoms of depression, anxiety and disruptive behaviour. Geelong Grammar School in Melbourne is playing a key role in the development of this approach to education in Australia.[41] Instead of encouraging interventions that aim simply to make a child 'feel better', the resiliency approach focuses on intervening to change a child's thinking about failure, encourage frustration-tolerance and reward persistence rather than mere success.

Many educators, including Nina Shokraii, are now advocating a return to a doing-well approach in the classroom. Encouragingly, the Department of Education in the UK seems to have moved in that direction already in its National Curriculum for personal, social and health education.[42] Psychologist Lauren Slater suggests:

> Maybe self-control should replace self-esteem as a primary peg to reach for ... Ultimately, self-control need not be seen as a constriction ... it might be experienced as the kind of practiced prowess an athlete or an artist demonstrates, muscles not tamed but trained, so that the leaps are powerful, the spine supple and the energy harnessed and shaped.[43]

It is encouraging to see that the limitations and dangers of the myth of self-esteem are being recognised, at least within certain segments of society. Signs of this awareness are emerging even within the pop-culture that has played such a significant role in generating the myth. Associated with this, I sense a yearning to reclaim from our past a more wholesome notion of self-esteem that goes hand in hand with self-respect. It is a yearning for self-esteem that is related to a 'virtuous' life, a life that is 'just and right', a life characterised by 'realistic self-evaluation' and by 'living responsibly and with integrity', breathing new life into words of wisdom written long ago.

I welcome this, yet long to go further. My yearning is that, in our ongoing exploration of this important issue, we place a greater emphasis on human spirituality and its potential impact on both the 'feeling good' and the 'doing well' aspects of self-esteem. I will revisit this topic in the final chapters of this book.

9

How Have We Become So Self-Oriented?

In just a few generations, in the Western world at least, we have eliminated much of the unpleasantness of life as experienced by our forebears. We can regulate the temperature and even the humidity of our homes, day and night, all year round – if we are prepared to pay for the privilege and ignore the environmental cost. Few of us have to endure pain or live under threat of death from a minor disease or accident. Nor do we have to trudge long distances daily, sleep on hard surfaces, draw water from wells or cut wood for cooking and heating.

We have enough leisure time and enough resources to be totally absorbed in and distracted by ourselves – our past, our present and our pretensions about the future. To avoid the challenges of relating to those who test our patience, our communication skills or our compassion, we can simply block them out with the ubiquitous iPod, mobile phone or other electronic device. When we shop, we no longer even have to look a checkout person in the eye – we can use a computerised self-service system or order groceries online and have them delivered to the door.

Despite the comfort and ease we experience, I believe that the loss of personal connection and the loss of challenge and rigour in everyday life are proving costly. I am not a Luddite, nor am I advocating a return to the hardship and lack of basic comforts and amenities of former times. What I want to do is to draw attention to factors that have impelled us towards an individualistic preoccupation with ourselves. This preoccupation has contributed to changes in our society that profoundly influence the way we think and live, and has provided the fertile ground that enabled self-esteem mythology to take root and flourish.

The all-about-me attitude that is so prevalent in today's society is not merely a recent pop-culture fad. We began moving in this direction long before the emergence of a recognisable self-esteem movement. As part of this process, we have changed in our thinking about how individuals function within society, and about motivation, work, profit, and human psychology and emotions. The ideas of some great thinkers of previous centuries, although appearing laudable at the time, can now be seen to have contributed to the present tendency to be preoccupied with ourselves.

Early influences

In the latter part of the eighteenth century, the Scottish philosopher and economist, Adam Smith, wrote a book about the nature and causes of wealth, which has been described as one of the most influential books ever written.[1] In it he expressed his then highly radical view that self-interest as a guiding principle could be a force for good within the world of commerce as well as the wider society.

It is important to note that Smith placed his ideas about self-interest carefully within the prevailing context of a moral framework of social responsibility. For example, he said that in the world of commerce there must be genuine, open competition and no coercion. Even more importantly, he had extremely idealistic views about the altruistic nature of humankind and believed that this would inevitably counterbalance any possible negative effects – on others or society – of choosing to pursue one's own interests. He wrote:

> How selfish soever man may be supposed, there are evidently some principles in his nature, which interest him in the fortune of others, and render their happiness necessary to him, though he derives nothing from it except the pleasure of seeing it.

Ralph Waldo Emerson, an influential American poet of the nineteenth century, also encouraged self-interest as a guiding principle in his transcendentalist essay 'On self-reliance'. However, in contrast to Smith, he did not regard altruism as an essential aspect of either human nature or society. Indeed he was highly critical of philanthropy. He is described as pre-empting the self-esteem movement in many ways:

> [Emerson] posits that the individual has something fresh and authentic within and that it is up to him to discover it and nurture it apart from the corrupting pressures of social influence ... Emerson never mentions 'self-esteem' in his essay, but his every word echoes with the self-esteem movement of today.[2]

Emerson's belief in self-reliance and the autonomy of the individual 'soul' was a liberating message against the background of intellectual tyranny and social manipulation of his day. In the context of our postmodern world, however, the over-zealous application of such perspectives has helped us on our path towards a radical individualism – an individualism in which ethics become a personal prerogative, and the welfare of others becomes a moral option rather than a social responsibility.

A contemporary of Emerson, the British philosopher John Stuart Mill, wrote a widely read essay entitled 'On liberty'; it was published in 1859 and is still in print today. Like Emerson, Mill emphasised the individual and the right to personal freedom rather than conformity to society or others, but he attempted to balance this by acknowledging the need for social responsibility. He introduced the 'harm principle – each individual has the right to act as they want, as long as the action does not harm others – a code widely used as a benchmark for moral behaviour today. Unfortunately, 'I can do what I want as long as I do not hurt others' may all too easily become 'I can do what I want because I have the right to do it'.[3]

Maslow's hierarchy of needs

For many people, the psychologist Abraham Maslow's name is synonymous with a pyramidal diagram representing his theory of the hierarchy of human needs. This appears, not only in books about psychology, but also in many motivational books and presentations in the business world. Maslow introduced his theory in a scholarly article in 1943, then presented it in a book entitled *Motivation and Personality* in 1954.[4]

Typically, 'esteem' appears near the pinnacle of the pyramidal hierarchy, surmounted only by 'self-actualisation'. According to Maslow's theory, as originally presented, these two paramount needs are the ones we will strive to satisfy once our more basic needs have been met. For him, esteem included stable self-esteem 'soundly based upon real capacity, achievement and respect from others', which he equated with self-respect. Self-actualisation he saw as fulfilling 'the desire to become more and more what one is, to become everything that one is capable of becoming'. Increased self-orientation is the perhaps unforeseen, but almost inevitable, consequence of the importance that Maslow's theory assigned to self-esteem and self-actualisation.

The counterculture of the 1960s

By the 1950s, a period of rapid social and technological change had left people somewhat bewildered. Because the consciousness of the culture was so utterly swamped by the trappings of progress, a significant minority of young people and some of their creative elders turned away from the prevailing culture. They intuitively revolted against materialism, rationalism and scientific reductionism, and the loss of community, mystery and spirituality. As historian Theodore Roszak writes, 'reductionist science, ecocidal industrialism, and corporate regimentation was too small a vision of life to lift the spirit'.[5]

The context of this emerging counterculture was unity and togetherness. Indeed, much of the search occurred in communes and alternative underground movements of close fellowship, beginning with the *beatniks* in the 1950s and extending to the *hippie* counterculture movements that flourished in the 1960s and 1970s. Yet, strangely, coexisting with this longing for connection was an intense search for self. The seeds of a rapid surge towards individualism were sown in the fields of hippie togetherness.

My present concern about the self-orientation promoted by self-esteem mythology has its roots in my interactions with the hippie counterculture. Much that it offered attracted me. The quest for community, the disdain of conspicuous consumption and greed, and the peaceful resistance to international aggression and war seemed like a candle flickering in the gathering gloom. But this quest for community was accompanied by an increasing emphasis on 'doing your own thing'. A self-oriented dysfunctional twin was born alongside the healthy child of free speech, desegregation, cultural diversity and the right to regulate one's own lifestyle.

A new sexual freedom, drugs, rock 'n' roll, and utopian politics served to liberate people from enslavement to rationalistic thinking. Some of us who worked amongst the counterculture of the 1960s and 1970s can give strong evidence that, for thousands of young people, experimentation with psychedelic drugs was initially a genuine attempt to escape the downside of modern living and enter a new and superior human consciousness.

Due to the rising power of the visual image through television, major historical and political issues such as the Vietnam War became traumatising. Many of my generation were forever impacted by just a handful of unforgettable images. Who could forget the fleeing Vietnamese child covered in burning napalm, or the South Vietnamese officer about to blow out the brains of a kneeling captive Vietcong? Revulsion against such horror contributed to widespread protests, especially among young people, which threatened to bring down the American government's determination.

At that time, students in the Western world believed political activism could change it all. In 1970, five years before the end of the war in Vietnam, a popular song by the folk-rock group Crosby, Stills, Nash and Young was challenging young people to change and rearrange the world, reinforcing the prevailing view. The refrain of their song 'Chicago' resonated strongly with the yearning of young people for a better world. The establishment turned out to be more resilient than expected, however, and the attempts to inspire a new, enlightened humanity through alternative communal lifestyles, consciousness-altering drugs and meditational techniques failed. Many disillusioned young people turned inwards, as tends to happen when our external world seems out of control or unreal.

Despite outward adherence to communal experience, many of those who had embraced the counterculture became obsessed with an individualistic search for spiritual enlightenment.[6] There was intense interest in meditation, and in Eastern religions and philosophy, as part of this journey. Following the Beatles' shift from drugs to transcendentalism, Zen, Hindu and Buddhist gurus were sought out by many prominent rock groups. For many, this 'spiritual' searching was little more than an alternative way of doing their own thing. I believe that this was, in essence, no different from the libertarian views presented by Emerson and Mill in the nineteenth century in terms of its primary focus on the isolated self.

The increased interest in Eastern religions gave momentum to the New Age movement, which brought together a hotchpotch of theologies, philosophies and superstitions from many sources, liberally laced with pseudoscience. This movement, like the counterculture, arose out of an intense inward search for personal 'truth'. While promoting universal togetherness and love, it was in fact highly individualistic in nature, making it almost impossible to define precisely. New Age notions of spirituality are still evident in the claims of many of the gurus of the myth of self-esteem.

In 1973, when I first visited Telegraph Avenue near Berkeley's University of California (a countercultural icon), the hippie experiment was in its death throes. As a structurally alternative society, the counterculture had already failed. However, it did not lose its power to reconfigure values and reshape institutions, with outcomes that were neither desired nor expected by the mainstream or alternative cultures of the day.[7] Probably no more than 5% of the hippie generation were committed to the radical social and political agenda and anti-materialism of the hippie activists.[8] However, it seems that many more bought into the radical individualistic focus on self that emerged during that period.

These major shifts towards individualism facilitated dissemination and popularisation of Maslow's ideas beyond academia and into the wider community, with varying degrees of distortion in the process. Under these favourable conditions, the simplistic notion that self-actualisation and self-esteem are the highest of human needs took root and spread rapidly throughout Western societies, reinforcing and further justifying our growing self-orientation.

The power of positive thinking

The conviction that repeating affirmations and mantras can build self-esteem or bring about desired outcomes, so beloved of Oprah and similar gurus, reflects in part the increased interest in Eastern religious practices that began in the 1950s. However, it also has deep roots in Western culture. In 1920, Émile Coué, a French pharmacist, introduced a method of autosuggestion as psychotherapy in his clinic. It was characterised by frequent repetition of a formula many of us will have heard: 'Every day, and in every way, I am becoming better and better.'

Similarly, Napoleon Hill, author of the 1937 classic *Think and Grow Rich*, became well known for the affirmation, 'What the mind can conceive and believe, it can achieve'. In other words, your thoughts control your destiny — you can be whatever you want to be. The enduring popularity of Hill's book, especially within the business community, has ensured its continued publication; it is still in print.

Hill's focus on the power of the mind has been echoed by many others over the years. It received particular impetus when Norman Vincent Peale's book *The Power of Positive Thinking* was released in 1952. Peale followed this with a string of bestsellers, including *Positive Imaging: The Powerful Way to Change Your Life* published 30 years later.[9] The ongoing popularity of his books, backed by his standing as the respected pastor of a mega-church in Manhattan, played a significant role in preparing the way for acceptance of self-esteem mythology. *You Can If You Think You Can*, a collection of stories of individual success against the odds, was another title that served as an inducement to believe the 'be-whatever-you-want-to-be' myth. Author and televangelist Robert Schuller, with his catchcry 'possibility thinking', was responsible in his heyday for spreading Peale's ideas to the vast audiences who viewed his TV show or read his books.[10]

I do not wish to condemn all of Peale's home-spun advice: who would argue with his encouragement to persevere in the face of obstacles, captured in the aphorism 'when life hands you a lemon, make lemonade'? But there is more than a hint of Coué's mind-over-matter autosuggestion in the repetitive techniques Peale advocated. There is also a pervasive emphasis on clinging tenaciously to positive, 'good' feelings and thoughts, irrespective of the circumstances, while blotting out supposedly harmful 'negative' thoughts or feelings. Embedded in this is the denial of reality, associated with the feel-good aspect of the myth of self-esteem.

Through the influence of Peale, Schuller and others who preached a doctrine of the seemingly limitless power of positive thinking, the focus on self advanced relentlessly from the secular world into the realm of religion.

Branden's emphasis on self-esteem

In 1969, Nathaniel Branden, whose influence on the development of the self-esteem movement has already been noted, presented self-esteem as a basic human need. The crucial importance he placed on self-esteem would have been sufficient in itself to move us further along the path to self-orientation. However, adding to this was his fervent belief in the autonomy of the individual, which was strongly antagonistic to the prevailing determinism of that time.

According to the deterministic view,[11] our personal histories and even global change were not shaped by free choice alone but primarily by biological, economic, psychological and historical forces. Our personal behaviour was no longer our choice but the result of genetic inheritance, sexual repression, childhood trauma, and social conditioning. The individual was no longer in control but rather a helpless victim of circumstances.

Branden went to an opposite extreme. He championed not only disconnected individualism but also individual freedom to make unfettered choices. He almost denied the power of cultural influences and dysfunctional nurturing to affect our ability to make good personal decisions. Uncritically accepting the latter view clearly leads in the direction of the be-whatever-you-want-to-be myth.

Branden was strongly influenced by his close association with philosopher Ayn Rand, who extolled 'the virtue of selfishness'.[12] Through her writings, in which she preached an extremely self-centred, greed-is-good form of laissez-faire capitalism, she had a profound impact on the business community in the USA and elsewhere. Her epic novels, *The Fountainhead* (1943) and *Atlas Shrugged* (1957), are still attracting readers. While Rand echoed Adam Smith in her promotion of individualistic self-interest, she rejected completely his emphasis on the need for an overarching moral commitment to social responsibility.

It was within Rand's philosophical framework that Branden developed his theories about self-esteem. Shared initially with other psychologists, they were soon being disseminated widely through books written for the popular market, beginning with *The Psychology of Self-Esteem*. Evidence of his lasting impact on public consciousness is the 2001 release of a 32nd Anniversary Edition of the latter book with the subtitle *A Revolutionary Approach to Self-Understanding that Launched a New Era in Modern Psychology*.[13]

In 1987, at about the same time as the government policy aimed at boosting self-esteem as a panacea for social ills was being adopted in California, Branden's book *How To Raise Your Self-Esteem* was released. Whether it was his intention or not, this book's title, taken together with its author's credentials, may well have served as an endorsement of that policy – a policy that was pivotal in spreading the self-esteem movement into both social institutions and popular culture. His elevation of self-esteem to the status of 'the single most important factor for a fulfilling life'[14] and his skill in communicating his ideas to the popular market played a significant part in propelling us towards self-focus.

Perhaps this outcome should not come as a surprise given that Branden held such radically individualistic views about the way we humans should function in society. Carol Craig argues that the concept of self-esteem as originally presented by Branden was not only distorted by his political and philosophical views but was also impractical and too intellectual.[15] Such flaws, she says, have led almost inevitably to the present trivialisation of this term and confusion about its meaning. Branden has since tried to correct current misconceptions about self-esteem, but the problem of an excessive focus on the self remains.[16]

The technological revolution

I marvel at the amazing advances in technology that have occurred in my lifetime, and I am quick to embrace the latest technology if I believe it is going to make me more effective in achieving my purposes. For all its many benefits, however, the technical revolution also has the potential to contribute in various ways to the individualism and lack of social cohesion that typify self-oriented societies. It can encourage us to live our lives 'one mile wide and one inch deep'.[17]

The power of the dynamic TV image and its globalisation through free enterprise have enabled ideas to be disseminated with unprecedented speed and global penetration. This, together with the advent of internet communication, has changed the way we think about ourselves and form our opinions about the world around us. It has enhanced our ability to form personalised worldviews out of the flotsam and jetsam of pop-culture ideas, rather than adopting classic big-picture ideologies.[18] Many of the ideas we assimilate are decidedly self-oriented. For some people, even the classic religions seem to have become so personalised that fundamental beliefs have been abandoned or revamped in order to accommodate their self-interest.

While enhanced communication has enriched our lives in many ways, it has also made us more vulnerable to distorted thinking about ourselves. It may also make it difficult for us to form the healthy connections with others that would counter this problem. As a young panellist on a TV show astutely commented, Facebook and Twitter allow you to look good without having to do good. 'I think it gives a lot of us an opportunity to present an image of ourself which isn't accurate,' he said.[19] In addition, the growing tendency for people to acquire large numbers of Facebook friends as status symbols and adopt multiple online personae must surely be encouraging a sense of self that is built on very shaky foundations.

Nicholas Carr, former executive editor of the *Harvard Business Review*, presents what he describes as a growing body of scientific evidence suggesting that the internet is turning us into scattered and superficial thinkers.[20] He says that when we are constantly distracted and interrupted – as we tend to be when looking at our computer or iPad screens, or connecting to others via mobile phones, Twitter and

Facebook – our brains cannot forge the strong and expansive neural connections that allow us to think deeply and creatively. The neuronal effects persist even when we are not actually using the technology. Eminent British neuroscientist Susan Greenfield is expressing similar concerns.[21] Moreover, heavy exposure to screen violence in adolescence may be changing the development of young people's brains in ways likely to lead to increased aggression, reckless behaviour and decreased empathy.[22] Ongoing research in this area is crucial.

In his book entitled *Present Shock*, Douglas Rushkoff describes as a 'destabilizing influence' an escalating tendency to compress time and space into the present moment.[23] As one manifestation of this, he says, individuals feel an increasing sense of urgency to keep abreast of what is happening as it is happening. This drives people to stay connected to a never-ending stream of digitised information but leaves no time between information downloads for them to reflect on what they are receiving or gain insight from it.

Any activity that reduces our capacity to engage in quieter, more attentive modes of thought that underpin contemplation, reflection and introspection – whether by modifying our brain networks or impacting our psyche – deprives us of the emotional and spiritual health that are facilitated by these solitary pursuits.

Contemplation, reflection and introspection are the very attributes that assist us to evaluate ourselves and situations accurately, make sound judgements, build deep relationships, think creatively and explore our spirituality. If our ability to do this is impeded, we will become even more vulnerable to the myth of self-esteem, with its shallow self-orientation. Perhaps the renewed interest in meditation and contemplative techniques and in seeking advice from life coaches and spiritual directors is a reaction to this escalation of superficial thinking.

A programmer for the Mozilla Foundation, when asked to comment about the pros and cons of the internet, answered:

> Social networking encourages people to have a greater number of much shallower friendships. Insofar as online interaction replaces real-world interaction, the internet is a negative force in the social world. I know what 15 of my friends had for breakfast, but I don't know whether any of them is struggling with major life issues ... If this trend continues, people in 2020 will have hundreds of acquaintances but very few friends.[24]

A recent university-based survey of 5000 social network users in Canada compared the effects on wellbeing of real-life and online friendships.[25] The researchers found that participants who had more real-life friends were much more likely to report a greater sense of wellbeing, even after taking into account factors such as income, demographics and personality differences. In contrast, the number of online friends seemed to have little, if any, impact on wellbeing.

I know from personal experience that a Facebook friend can 'unfriend' you at the drop of a hat, for very trivial reasons or no apparent reason at all. In any case, whether we communicate electronically or in person, how many deep friendships is it possible to nurture? Probably no more than you could count on the fingers of one hand. The development of meaningful connections that are the basis of deep friendships takes time and commitment – uninterrupted time and undivided attention. How can we hope to achieve this while hooked up to an iPod or otherwise engaged in multitasking?

> We enjoy continual connection but rarely have each other's full attention ... We defend connectivity as a way to be close, even as we effectively hide from each other.[26]

Satisfying relationships are also characterised by trust, an unselfish commitment to our friend's best interests and the intimacy of a unique shared history. For example, I need to know that I can trust my friend to respect my privacy if I choose to share something deeply personal with them in confidence. Contrast this with the

How Have We Become So Self-Oriented?

now common practice of sharing personal information with all and sundry through social networking, or engaging in explicit phone conversations on public transport. This is not the way to build intimate friendships.

I am genuinely concerned that the technology that is revolutionising the way we connect with each other may, at the same time, be fostering disconnection from others and turning us inward. A strangely incongruent mix of *disengaged individualism* and *global togetherness* has become a significant characteristic of our times.

What can we do?

Once we are aware that the malady of self-orientation is afflicting us, it is important to start looking for a cure. In keeping with the age in which we live – the age of the quick fix and the punchy list of simplistic solutions – I am offering my list of practical steps that may help counter self-focus as possible starting points for personal change. However, I believe there are also important big-picture issues that cannot be captured in a few dot points such as these:

- Give up selective reading of popular gurus for a month.
- Take a month's break from TV shows promoting self-focused attitudes and material success.
- Try to think less of yourself for a month and more of the welfare of others; develop the more altruistic aspects of your mind and lifestyle.
- Read a biography of someone known for their contribution to the social, spiritual and cultural advancement of others; read *Tuesdays with Morrie,* or study the life and teachings of Jesus.[27]
- Watch an inspiring movie or TV series that places value on a life lived for others.
- Evaluate your strengths realistically; if necessary, stop trying to fill a role that does not match your aptitudes and personality.
- Focus on your 'blessings' more than your achievements – for

example, keep a gratitiude diary for a month.
- Find one or more friends who are humble and loving, and spend more time talking to them.
- Build sustainable, mutually nurturing and respectful relationships.

Like the proverbial frog in the kettle, who was boiled alive because he failed to notice that the temperature of the water around him was gradually rising, many of us have simply been unaware of the enormity of the threat posed by the pervasive spread of self-esteem mythology.

But it is worth reminding ourselves that we are not dealing with an inexorable force. Recognising these unsubstantiated myths and acknowledging their ability to wreak havoc in our lives and societies is, in itself, a useful first step towards bringing about change. A sociological myth such as the myth of self-esteem is 'a collective belief that is built up in response to the wishes of the group rather than an analysis of the basis of the wishes'.[28] It develops over time by the collective action of many individuals. It can be eradicated in similar fashion. Each individual who rejects even one aspect of self-esteem mythology is playing a part in laying it to rest. My earnest hope is that the myth-busting facts and alternative worldviews presented in this book will assist in the achievement of this goal.

10

The Impact of Self-Esteem Myths on Society

I have already highlighted many ways in which self-esteem myths are harming us individually and relationally. In this chapter, I focus on issues I see as particularly important to society as a whole.

All-about-me consumerism and politics

In 1979, former US President Jimmy Carter, in a powerful speech from the Oval Office, declared that the nation was at a turning point in its history, with two paths before it.[1] He issued a strong warning against moving from 'a path of common purpose' to 'the path that leads to fragmentation and self-interest' and saw disturbing signs that this was already happening. 'Too many of us now tend to worship self-indulgence and consumption. Human identity is no longer defined by what one does, but by what one owns,' he said.

Less than two years later, the USA took a major step towards conspicuous consumption under its new President Ronald Reagan and his Treasury Secretary Don Regan. The latter, as immediate past-Chairman of Merrill Lynch & Co, had close ties with Wall Street. A period of self-focused, market-driven, 'greed-is-good' politics began. This led ultimately to the disastrous collapse of Enron in 2001 and the ensuing global financial crisis, the effects of which are still being felt in the USA and around the world.

While consumption-driven politics is not unique to the USA, we need to acknowledge that this nation plays a pivotal role in shaping global attitudes. Cultural trends in the USA, whose citizens represent only 4.5% of the world population, have dominated world opinion in many respects, and continue to do so. Two major factors contributing to this dominance are the USA's economic power and its ability to influence popular culture through global media networks.

Many people now believe we are living on a planet that is in crisis, substantially because of global greed and the failure to examine the long-term consequences of our consumptive lifestyles. Well-known ecologist David Suzuki is one among many decrying the foolishness of regarding nature as an eternally abundant resource and clinging to notions of progress that require limitless growth and limitless expansion.[2]

US economist Robert H. Frank has expressed his concern about growing income inequality: as incomes increase over time, it is the already highly paid who are receiving the greatest share in his country.[3] This sets up an unhelpful cascade of events, where the purchasing power of those who are the wealthiest sets the norm for those below them on the income ladder, causing a progressive rise in expectations for those on the next rung down, and so on. The end result is that it is much harder for those on average and lower incomes to achieve what they have come to accept as their basic financial goals.

Working harder and longer to keep up with increasing expectations is exhausting. It leaves us anxious, resentful and irritable, and it robs us of time to do the things that bring lasting pleasure, such as spending time with friends and family or reading books that enrich us.⁴ Self-esteem mythology, with its tendency to invite delusional expectations in the quest for feeling good and 'following your dream', obviously feeds right into this problem.

The bias in Australia has also increasingly favoured the wealthy, and more so as greed and personal advantage have become central to our morality. Economic morality has been reduced to obligations towards investors. For example, workers on low incomes, and even many in well-paid professions, face constant job insecurity because of widespread downsizing, often undertaken simply to ensure increased profit margins. Similarly, those chasing fast profits by investing in the housing market care little about the rental crisis this causes for those on more limited incomes. Where self-interest reigns as a first consideration, such outcomes are inevitable.

The entry into the share market of the average middle-class citizen has caused a dramatic swing in political attitudes. Both legislators and voters, focused on share profits or a budget surplus, abandon issues such as a fair wage structure, the needs of indigenous people or refugees, international aid or even our threatened environment. It is very easy to find ourselves simply accepting the political and economic positions that will support our preferred lifestyle.⁵

I do want to stress again that being interested in yourself and in the prosperity of your own family or your own nation is not essentially wrong. However, this needs to be balanced by a conscious awareness of how much we have received from beyond ourselves, in one way or another. Losing sight of this important fact can seriously erode our sense of moral responsibility, not only to our families and relationships but also our national and global communities.

I read recently that some of the wealthiest people in the world, including the world's third-richest man Warren Buffet, are now offering to make special tax contributions to help resolve the problems of huge world debt in the wake of the global financial crisis in Europe and the USA.⁶ I sincerely hope that this is a heartening sign of a move away from the all-about-me attitudes that have marred the past.

Manipulative marketing

The willingness of Western societies to embrace self-esteem mythology in its various manifestations has left us wide open to exploitation by those who stand to gain by our consumption. A distorted perception of our needs is artificially devised and stimulated by profit-driven market forces that do not give a hoot about long-term consequences for the individual, the family, our health or our social cohesion.

The gap between our perceived needs and our real needs is being widened by gigantic advertising resources, for which the consumer pays. Clive Hamilton sees the market as complicit in encouraging us towards 'a particular form of individualism', in which pleasure gained by satisfying needs manufactured by the market becomes the purpose of life. He writes: 'The market now even offers us our identity – both our self-definition and the persona presented to the outside world – something previously determined by our place in the community.'[7]

The power of advertising is not simply its power to sell a product, but rather the power to instil changing values. We see social behaviour being constructed culturally to the advantage of the market and to the disadvantage of society. Richard Eckersley is convinced the 'media marketing complex is creating an "artificial" or "alternative" reality that is increasingly influential'.[8] He describes as 'cultural fraud' the widespread promotion of images and ideals that are at odds with psychological needs and social realities.

As an undesirable extension of aggressive marketing practices, we now see the cultures of developing countries becoming the focus of a massive industry to intrigue and entertain the Western world. Whereas colonists of bygone eras were dismissive of indigenous cultures or saw such cultural diversity as an impediment to their conquests, today we see an emergence of 'economic colonists' who now regard cultural novelty as a resource to be exploited. US economist and political advisor Jeremy Rifkin describes this as the 'strip-mining' of cultures.[9] For today's neo-colonialists, the purpose of understanding culture is not ultimately to respect it. Rather, it is to respect it only to the extent necessary to allow exploitation of its tourist potential or gain an advantage for whatever product is to be imposed upon the local people.

The irony is that most people who innocently enjoy reading articles or watching TV shows about distinctive global cultures, or visiting them, are unaware that the self-serving market forces driving this source of entertainment are in danger of compromising and destroying the very cultures that intrigue them.

Indifference to injustice

I find myself solidly onside with the opinion that wealth generation is not of itself at all evil. However, if commercial goals ignore social considerations, they beget injustice and will ultimately weaken civil society. In a just society, wealth generation is not only about maximising profits and returns on investments. It is also about the fair remuneration of those who have contributed their toil or intellectual capital and about the impact of such activities on the planet.

The marriage of wealth, prosperity and market-driven values to the feel-good self-esteem model, as celebrated by a myriad motivational spruikers, has seen social responsibility become overridden by the goal of personal achievement. We increasingly begrudge, and in some cases go to great lengths to dodge, paying the necessary taxes out of our affluence that would help meet the needs of those who struggle. The common practice of blaming the strugglers for causing their own problems helps us justify our indifference, but it fails to acknowledge that life can be hard for some people through no fault of their own.

We may ease our consciences by supporting benevolent organisations, leaving this issue to the Salvation Army, St Vincent de Paul and similar charities. We can even experience a feel-good rush as we make sporadic donations, which may be miniscule compared with what we spend on ourselves.

Because of my extensive involvement with marginalised people and my deep love and concern for them, I cannot ignore issues of social injustice when I write or speak publicly. I cannot ignore the stark contrast I see between the lavish, self-indulgent lifestyles encouraged by self-esteem mythology and the day-to-day reality experienced by many I encounter. Even in our affluent Western societies, many people live in abject poverty. In other parts of the world, many live in unspeakable conditions of disadvantage.

According to United Nations (UN) data, additional aid equivalent to US$40 billion was all that would have been required in 1998 to ensure that all those living in developing countries had access to basic education, health care, nutrition, water and sanitation.[10] To put this in perspective, $40 billion is considerably less than the total amount spent in that same year on perfumes, pet foods and ice-creams in Europe and the USA. Leisure, which once was the prerogative of the rich, is now normative across all classes. Many ordinary people now spend amounts on their leisure activities that would seem like winning a lottery to the other two-thirds of the world's population.

In September 2000 at UN Headquarters in New York, world leaders took a positive step when they committed their nations to a new global partnership to reduce extreme poverty. The UN Millennium Declaration they adopted listed eight Millennium Development Goals, all with a target deadline of 2015.[11] These ranged from halving extreme poverty to halting the spread of HIV/AIDS and providing universal primary education.

In September 2010, despite the global financial downturn, a previously agreed target for overseas aid was reaffirmed at a UN summit in New York – 0.7% of gross national income by 2015 for developed countries.[12] To our shame, this target was first set by the UN in 1970, 40 years earlier, with the goal of achieving it by the middle of that decade![13] By 2012, the contributions of more than two-thirds of developed countries, including wealthy nations such as the USA, Canada and Australia, had not reached the intermediary target of 0.5%, making it unlikely that they will achieve the 0.7% goal by 2015.[14]

Because aid is not always directed in the most effective ways towards the alleviation of poverty, comparing overall contributions does not tell the whole story.[15] Self-interest is again a factor. For example, in many cases, 'aid is primarily designed to serve the strategic and economic interests of the donor countries or to benefit powerful domestic interest groups'.[16] In addition, aid may not reach the countries that most desperately need it. Once received it may be distributed or spent inefficiently, or eaten away by endemic corruption.

Sadly, when it comes to alleviating global poverty, we have to acknowledge that most attempts to translate high sounding promises into reality have met with dismal failure in the past. If, for the sake of the world's poor, we want to achieve better outcomes in the future, we will need to move beyond current self-oriented policy making. As Mahatma Gandhi reminded us, 'The earth provides enough to satisfy every man's need, but not every man's greed.' Jeremy Sachs, in his classic book *The End of Poverty: How We Can Make it Happen in Our Lifetime*, presents compelling arguments that support this contention.[17]

It seems that we in the West are unwilling to accept limitations on our own excessive consumption in the interests of global justice or even the survival of the poor. We may admire, yet hide behind, the remarkable generosity of the few great humanitarians who bless every culture and age. For example, Bono, lead singer of U2, has been pressuring world leaders for many years to increase aid, cancel the debt of the world's poorest countries and improve terms of trade with them.[18] More than 100 of the world's wealthiest people have now pledged to give billions to humanitarian causes.[19] I live in hope that all of them will fulfil their promises. For the majority, however, our great fortune in the West has not been accompanied by a growing concern for those beyond our own small circle of family, friends and colleagues.

I am firmly convinced that, if lasting change is to occur, individuals as well as governments and wealthy philanthropists need to step up and take responsibility as part of the global community. However, this will require ordinary citizens like us to change our attitudes. In the present climate, can you imagine a political party campaigning on a policy of introducing an 'end global poverty' levy of say 1–2% on everyone earning a comfortable income? Would you vote for them if they did? Yet the actual personal cost, if we were to agree globally and concurrently to act to end poverty, is amazingly small.

Some individuals do give of themselves – as well as their creativity, skills and possessions – in extraordinarily self-denying ways. Magnificent human generosity can be displayed when catastrophes strike. Earthquakes, fires, floods and personal tragedies often generate an amazing response. Even where these funds cover the costs of dealing with the crisis, however, they have a negligible effect on addressing endemic poverty. They may not even be adequate to meet immediate needs unless helped along by celebrities taking up the cause.

If you would like to be part of making a difference, there are many options for you to explore.[20] Have you ever considered foregoing a small luxury, even a cup of barista-brewed coffee each week, and giving the equivalent as a donation to a local or international aid organisation? What about volunteering your services in your own locality or, if you are in a position to do so, a brief interstate or overseas placement working for an aid agency? There is a particular need for volunteers who can offer essential specialised skills.[21]

Many people remain oblivious or indifferent to the fact that we are putting self-interest before the interests of the poor when we pay relatively low prices for goods produced by poorly paid workers. In many cases, the low prices we enjoy are the result of deals between authoritarian governments and great multinational corporations. The hard question for us is this: would we be prepared to pay higher prices for goods if we knew that this would ensure a fair

The Impact of Self-Esteem Myths on Society

wage for impoverished workers in other countries? How different the world would be if prosperity and success were redefined in terms of communal values that made personal and corporate wealth at the expense of others unconscionable.

Let us embrace our mutual responsibility for the vast number of human beings whose most pressing problem is not a lack of self-esteem but a lack of the very basics of life necessary for survival. I find it impossible to fathom how we can remain so obsessed with ourselves and our self-esteem in such a world at such a time. How can we in all honesty feel good about ourselves, while closing our eyes to the masses of other humans living in misery? Facing and questioning the widening gap between the haves and have-nots is far from a negative we must avoid so we can go on feeling good; it is a challenge leading to a greater, healthier sense of true humanity.

Unbalanced communal positivity

We live in an era that attempts to minimise discomfort at every level. We are taught to evade uncomfortable or pessimistic thoughts and utterances at all cost, and we are bombarded with messages advocating positive thinking.[22]

As already noted, having a well-founded positive or optimistic attitude to life can be extremely helpful. However, it becomes potentially dangerous when it is out of touch with reality and not balanced by the tempering caution of pessimism. Blunting warranted (appropriate) sadness and anxiety increases the risk of 'unwarranted depression'.[23]

When unbalanced positivity prevails, the critical voice, the prophetic voice or the analytically realistic voice is ignored or vilified as negative. The so-called negative thinker may even be pitied as a person of low self-esteem. Some of us have been issuing unpopular warnings about the state of the global environment since the late 1960s. Now that the evidence of global degradation and consequent global climate change is mounting, the voice is heard, though still shrilly decried by a small minority.

Similarly, early this century in the lead up to the collapse of Enron and the corporate banking crisis, the voices that sounded warnings about highly speculative investment strategies and monetary policies were drowned out by the unfettered positivity of market entrepreneurs. If we encourage only positivity in our corporate cultures, this kind of tragedy will be all too common. When pessimistic criticism is so ridiculed that the essential whistleblower is eliminated and company irregularities hidden, many innocents suffer.

Children placed at risk

Inevitably, our children will be influenced by our value systems and beliefs, which in turn are the result of cultural information and social pressure. How else can we understand the compliance of ordinary German youth with the horror of the Holocaust? German children were made of the same stuff as our children. Racist messages in, racist children out. Self-oriented messages in, self-centred children out.

Children's literature, movies and TV are powerful vehicles for promulgating self-esteem mythology, both overtly and in subtle ways. The importance of parental monitoring of the books our children read and the TV shows and movies they watch, as well as their use of social-networking and mobile-phone technology, cannot be overstated.

> *At Concern Australia, we experienced the influence of self-esteem mythology on the Australian education system when we were forced to make significant changes to the format of our popular and highly effective Values4Life high school program. The difficulty we faced was that the public educational system was no longer interested in a values program that deals with a person's worldview in terms of religious and ethical belief systems. Our team must now be seen to address behavioural issues instead. Seminars on bullying, self-esteem or sexuality and relationships have replaced the critical analysis of our culture.*

Our presenters are skilled in youth issues and entertaining in their presentations, so we are still given rave reviews. But sadly, instead of confronting the larger issues of life in the context of finding meaning and purpose, we have to deal with behavioural outcomes rather than the causes. Since we are there by invitation and must comply, we – and more importantly, the students – have become victims of the current preoccupation with self-esteem.

The most vulnerable objects of our experiments based on defective notions of self-esteem are our children. And if a generation is misguided by well-meaning parents and educators, their children in turn will be scarred, even if the pendulum swings to another extreme in compensation. It is vitally important for us to question current conventional wisdom in order to protect our children. We need to be slow to send them down unexamined mineshafts of social theory to test the atmosphere, like the canaries used by Welsh miners to test the levels of toxic gas. It just may be that, unwittingly, we have been placing our children in danger – with narcissism, aggression, chronic depression, even suicide, as worst-case scenarios – by promoting unrealistic expectations and isolating them from healthy relationships and a nobler vision that looks beyond themselves.

Celebrity adulation

Another, perhaps unexpected, outcome of the myth of self-esteem is a widespread fascination with celebrity. What someone wears to a TV or sporting awards night, movie premiere or horse race now seems to be a matter of intense interest. Even traditional churchgoers I know are deeply and emotionally attached to cable TV gossip shows, and many people enter avidly into the fantasy life offered by so-called reality TV. More emotion can be evoked by a criticism of this plastic world of ego-obsession than discussion of the great political and social controversies of our day.

This societal trend bears many of the hallmarks of self-esteem mythology. I see the unquestioning adulation celebrities attract, irrespective of the appropriateness of their behaviour, as an extreme example of the disjunction between feeling good and doing well that is at the heart of distorted teaching about self-esteem. Celebrity adulation may also be a response to the call to associate ourselves with people and situations that keep us feeling good. A society that hypes up its expectations of normality by feeding on the lifestyles of celebrities is heading along a dangerous path.

Finding our balance

As so often happens, in the face of one extreme, another extreme is born. In reaction to oppressive determinism of earlier times, many in Western societies have embraced an extreme form of individualism that is destructive to both the individual and society. An influential part of this process appears to have been a rush to judgement in favour of the self-esteem movement. Its distorted notions of self and self-esteem are now entrenched in modern Western societies, almost from the cradle to the grave.

For those of us who have lived through the twentieth century's banal 1950s, the experimental 1960s and 1970s and the greed-is-good era that began in the late 1980s, the speed of change over that period has been unimaginable. More importantly, the direction of the changes that have occurred were rarely prophesied. Who could have imagined, for example, that the longing for peace during my youth would give way to the current political acceptance of pre-emptive war?

Perhaps it is partly in reaction to the collectivism of communism and the disaster it produced in the violation of individual rights and enterprise that we have become so self-oriented and have so greatly elevated individual freedom and self-determination. The issue is no longer whether something can be proven to be true objectively, but *how it is perceived by me* and *how it will impact my life*. Aided by a massively financed pop-culture blitz, we have, within a few decades, swept aside centuries of belief in the individual's responsibility to play a part in the transformation of society as a whole.

With the abandonment of the communal dream, we are losing our ability to function as healthy communities at the local, national and global level. The seriousness of this loss is obscured by the celebration of the new freedom to do as we please and the seductive increase in lifestyle diversions. This is facilitated, for the majority, by above-subsistence incomes and access to advanced technology. It would be foolish to attempt to place the entire blame for our present state of detached self-orientation at the feet of the self-esteem movement. However, there is no doubt in my mind that this movement has given enormous impetus to our journey inwards by providing ready-made, widely accepted justifications for such self-focus.

By our very nature as human beings, I believe, we now find ourselves struggling to come to grips with a fundamental dichotomy. We are virtually hardwired to experience two conflicting realities.

First, *we are self-conscious and intensely self-aware.* Whether by design or development, we are creatures acutely aware of our own being. I believe the rapid uptake and persistence of the self-esteem movement is related to this – it hooks into the distinctively human attribute of self-consciousness. It is hardly surprising then that unsubstantiated claims about the importance of self-esteem found receptive ears. In a sense, we are primed to accept Nathaniel Branden's influential claims that 'positive self-esteem is a basic human need ... indispensable to normal and healthy development'.[24] If a cultural message stresses self-esteem as a primary function, it will become a self-fulfilling prophecy. Inevitably, the quest for self-esteem will seem compelling.

Second, *we are social creatures whose health and welfare is not found in self-fulfilment.* Physical comfort, safety and material wellbeing do not alone satisfy this inner awareness. This has found expression in the impressive numbers of contemplative and visionary thinkers who have written, and continue to write, about the dangers of individualism, materialism, consumerism and secularism.

If we accept these two statements as human reality, it follows that the symptoms of dissatisfaction in the midst of plenty in Western societies, in their many guises, may not be caused by a lack of self-esteem but rather by the lack of a bigger picture, a meaningful life and an outward journey away from the tyranny of self. However, the volume of self-esteem proclamation can all too easily drown out the inherent intuitive message: *it is not all about me!*

The inflated ego and the depressed ego are not the only possibilities. Beyond the two extremes of self-indulgence and self-denigration lies a liberating possibility: self-transcendence. I would like to shout from the rooftops the deep joy of experiencing an awareness of others, the fulfilment that comes from finding our true place in the scheme of things, and the beauty and creativity that this releases. I want people to know it is possible to shift our gaze away from our own needs and find deep satisfaction in meaningful work, relationships and human existence.

11

Finding Identity and Meaning

Under the influence of self-esteem mythology, Western notions of identity, meaning and spirituality have been shaped by the growing emphasis on the individual as the primary point of reference. These are the themes I address in this chapter and the remaining chapters of this book.

The quest for meaning

Despite the cynicism of the classic Monty Python movie *The Meaning of Life*, with its perceptive lampooning of both secular and god-bothering approaches to the topic, a genuine quest for meaning remains central to health and motivation for most of us. Is the purpose of life really to find myself? Or is there something more?

> Situated on the Gold Coast is one of the more select and expensive of Queensland's private secondary schools. Some time ago, Concern Australia's Values4Life team was invited to spend a week there, presenting seminars on the theme 'Values, Relationships, Australian Culture and Spirituality'. We were also given free access to any students who wanted personal time with us.

Beyond the Myth of Self-Esteem

> *Everything in that school had the scent of excellence and success. Class time radiated the students' corporate eagerness to learn and the teachers' profound commitment. However, all was not well. Here is a rather extreme example of the problems we encountered.*
>
> *Nathan (not his real name) came to me deeply distressed. Seconds into our conversation he was in tears. This in essence is what he told me: 'My parents are very rich. They give me everything I could wish for as far as things go. They recently sent me to the Bahamas for a holiday with plenty of cash to spend. I know that if I do well in school, they'll give me a luxury car when I leave next year. But they hate each other and all I ever hear is bitter and angry conversations between them. They are so busy making money that they don't have a lot of time to spend with me. Anyway, I think they've got so many problems of their own, they don't have time to talk outside of that. I have everything a young bloke could ever want but, please, tell me who I am. I have no idea who I am.'*

It was his story, and many similar stories we heard during school visits over several decades, that stirred a deep desire in me to understand the nature of human self-awareness and the distortions and agonies that can be associated with the search for identity, meaning and fulfilment in life. This desire was reinforced when I listened to one of the most popular songs at that time, 'The Logical Song' by Supertramp, who were echoing the heart cry of young people: 'Who am I?.[1]

Despite the widespread adoption of lifestyle choices and techniques that are supposed to bring us happiness and satisfaction, a significant proportion of people are not feeling hugely positive about themselves or the context in which they live. Why is there not an overwhelming sense of gratitude and contentment when, for most of us, the conditions under which we live are socially, politically and materially superior to those of almost all the humans beings who have ever existed? Why is the widespread impression of progress not delivering broadly experienced satisfaction with life and society?

Is looking after my house, my kids, my family and myself, too small a deal? Is the human spirit destined for something far greater than self-interest? I firmly believe that it is. This is an issue I have been passionate about for a long time. I first wrote about it more than 20 years ago in a book entitled *Advance Australia Where? A Lack of Meaning in a Land of Plenty*.[2]

In Western societies generally, an increasing malaise of personal identity has accompanied the materialistic perspective that gives secondary significance to social and spiritual meaning. Ironically, it is this increasing focus on self that so often leads to a diminution of the person. As a consequence, regaining a sense of identity and purpose has become a serious issue. The fact that a book entitled *The Purpose Driven Life: What on Earth Am I Here For?* maintained No. 1 position in *The New York Times*' bestseller list for two years, and has now sold more than 30 million copies, suggests that the author was on to something.[3]

Clive Hamilton is convinced that people are hungry to live with purpose, in ways that are consistent with the construction of a more ethical, just, sustainable and peaceful society.[4] He is but one of the many who, like myself, believe that the desire for a meaningful life is deeply embedded in the modern and postmodern heart.

A deeper kind of happiness

The ancient Greek philosopher Aristotle taught that the ideal life was the life of *eudaimonia*, a word usually translated as 'happiness'. However, Aristotle was certainly not talking about a life of sensory pleasure, or a life so disengaged from the real world that it avoids any painful realities. His kind of happiness incorporated the idea of living well. By this he meant living in accordance with reason, fulfilling one's sense of purpose, doing one's civic duty, living virtuously, being fully engaged with the world and, in particular, experiencing the richness of human love and friendship.[5]

Clinical psychologist Timothy Sharp (Dr Happy) has suggested the following as ways of 'choosing' happiness:

C - clarity of goals, direction and life purpose
H - healthy living, including exercise, diet and sleep
O - optimistic, positive but realistic thinking
O - others: developing and enjoying key relationships in life
S - strengths: identifying, improving and utilising strengths
E - enjoying the moment, living in and appreciating the present.[6]

This list does contain some common-sense advice that may help us get more enjoyment out of life – but, in my view, it is sadly lacking when it comes to helping us find meaning and the deeper kind of happiness Aristotle had in mind. The *feeling good* aspect of happiness seems to be considered without any reference to the notion of *doing good* for others. In fact, others are mentioned only as a source of enjoyment for oneself.

Strangely, it seems that the more we seek happiness, the less likely we are to find it. Indeed, Viktor Frankl saw the phrase 'the pursuit of happiness', which is enshrined in the United States Declaration of Independence, as a contradiction in terms.[7] He said happiness cannot be *pursued*. Happiness *ensues* as a by-product of dedication to a task, a cause or a person other than yourself. Asking ourselves '"How can I become happier?" is a classic sign that we have missed the point,' writes Hugh Mackay. '"How can I be more useful?" might be getting warm.'[8]

Martin Seligman agrees that pursuing happiness directly will not lead to greater life satisfaction. He recommends discovering what your highest strengths are and then using them to belong to and serve something you believe is larger than the self.[9] He is convinced that we need something bigger to inspire us and sustain us.

An interesting series entitled *Making Australia Happy* was presented on ABC TV in 2010. Eight ordinary people from one of Australia's 'most miserable areas' were filmed while undergoing an eight-week program of scientifically developed exercises aimed at helping them 'find greater fulfilment and meaning in their lives'. In one intriguing exercise, participants were each given $20 and left at a shopping mall under instruction to use the money to make a stranger happy. Another task was aimed at deepening the individual's social connections. For most participants, 'happiness' appeared to rise substantially throughout the program.

Any positive changes in participants in a program such as this are to be commended, yet I am left wondering whether such changes will last. Furthermore, while some of the exercises certainly encouraged connecting with others, the primary motivation seemed to be merely a self-serving desire to feel happier, an attitude that is all too common.[10] Surely, this too falls far short of achieving the deeper kind of happiness that Aristotle envisaged.

'Bread alone' is not enough

Richard Eckersley has claimed that 'the more materialistic we are, the poorer our quality of life'.[11] One of the central tenets of the counterculture of the 1960s was a belief that a truly happy, fruitful individual or a wholesome society could not be produced by materialism alone. Although at times I have wavered a little from that view, I am now convinced it is true. As Jesus said, 'People do not live by bread alone'. We cannot live happily by mountains of bread, by the finest of bread, by unique bread or by multitudes of bread options. Clive Hamilton writes:

> Like all humans, what modern Australians want above all is for their lives to have purpose. But finding meaning is not easy, especially when people are subjected to a barrage of commercial messages that promote superficiality, self-deception and laxity.[12]

> Some have found promising paths in spiritual traditions or psychological 'work', but most have ended up seeking a proxy identity in the form of commodity consumption. People continue to pursue greater wealth and consume at ever-higher levels

because they do not know how better to answer the question 'How should I live?'[13]

According to Hamilton, research shows consistently that those who set themselves intrinsic goals (for example, strong relationships and contributing to the community) have greater life satisfaction than those who set themselves external goals (for example, wealth, fame and sexual conquests).[14] This view is also supported by a long-term study of life satisfaction, in which more than 60,000 people participated.[15] A key finding was that people who increased their 'social participation' (that is, how often they met with, or did something to help, friends, relatives or neighbours) showed corresponding gains in satisfaction and vice versa. Another large-scale study, across many cultures, has indicated that 'the reward experienced from helping others may be so deeply ingrained in human nature' as to be regarded as a 'psychological universal'.[16]

Helpful role models

My father and grandfather were extremely fulfilled, basically happy, psychologically healthy individuals. They both loved fishing, cricket and football. They enjoyed nature and gardening. They were innovative and creative, and voracious readers of almost everything. It never occurred to them that they should fixate on themselves, their own needs or their own happiness. They were not without their faults, and I believe these previous generations were too lavish in their censure of failure and too restrained in encouragement and recognition of effort and success. But they were not self-indulgent: they certainly functioned less self-destructively than following generations, and without the self-oriented cravings so prevalent today.

I feel grateful to have had the privilege of meeting others over the years who never seemed to be preoccupied with their level of happiness or life satisfaction – truly impressive people, high achievers by any standards. They expressed a sense of humanity, a conviction that

Finding Identity and Meaning

life is worth living and a commitment to significant issues. This raises the question: are people like this happy? For instance, were Mother Theresa, Martin Luther King Jr or Mahatma Ghandi happy? Or were they something greater than happy?

If you were to ask me whether I am happy, I am not sure what that is supposed to mean. I spend much of my time sharing in the pain of broken people. This is hardly the stuff of happiness, but it is certainly a significant and meaningful pursuit when one sees the healing and transformation that come through care.

In the 1990s, I was invited to attend a conference in Atlanta, Georgia, which brought together people in leadership who were deeply committed to working with the urban poor. Although a prosperous city with the largest airport in the USA, Atlanta had developed ghettos far worse than anything most of us could imagine. The conference was convened by Robert Lupton, founder and president of FCS Urban Ministries, a charismatic visionary who was the driving force behind a number of transformational inner-city programs for Atlanta.[17]

The speaker at one of the sessions was one of the most powerful men in the city, a millionaire who described himself as 'a chain-smoking lapsed Catholic'. He said his life had been changed dramatically through meeting Lupton. Radiating joy, he told us about several successful projects that had been implemented as a result.

One of his stories was about Atlanta's old gaol, a huge concrete monolith that had housed more than 500 inmates. Some time after it closed in 1995, Lupton proposed to the city leaders that it could be refurbished and converted into a centre for transients and homeless people. As a starting point, he called together architects and others from the community who could provide resources relevant to urban construction – in fact, anyone who could potentially contribute to a project of this magnitude was invited. Some were religious, many were not, but his proposal captured their imagination. The gaol site was purchased by a generous donor and deeded to the Metro Atlanta Task Force for the Homeless, and wealthy people in the community were inspired to give

147

generously to finance the project. This site now provides shelter and services to an average of 1,000 men, women, and children on a daily basis.[18]

So great was the sense of fulfilment engendered by such projects that highly skilled people actively sought involvement in similar ventures. With the mayor of the city's support, a dark, criminal-infested ghetto area wedged under a highway in a disused railway system was transformed into a marketplace. It became one of the most attractive multicultural centres in the city, where both black and white residents of the surrounding neighbourhoods could buy and sell all manner of goods at an affordable price.[19] *In this new setting, people who were previously 'losers' were able to succeed.*

Another project involved providing decent homes in one of the worst suburbs in Atlanta, where drug lords used to cruise around with impunity. This was funded by setting up a luxury golf course in another area and charging wealthy patrons a membership fee of $100,000. Eventually, through concerted direct action by the newly empowered women of the community, the drug lords were driven out of the rebuilt area.

Our speaker, who played a major role in coordinating these projects, was nearly jumping out of his skin with enthusiasm as he spoke to us: 'Once I had become involved in being part of the transformation of the city, making another million dollars meant nothing to me. I have never before found such fulfilment and happiness as I now find in being part of the answer to the city's problems — through giving my talent, my finance and my time to this reclamation of human lives.'

Few of us will be able to match the impressive skills and resources that this man brought to these projects. Nevertheless, whatever our level of giftedness, we can all draw inspiration from his willingness to take action. Bengali poet Rabindranath Tagore, a Nobel laureate and friend of Ghandi, once wrote:

> I slept and dreamt that life was joy.
> I awoke and saw that life was service.
> I acted and behold, service was joy.

How perceptive. How profound.

An inherent need for meaning

In my extensive reading of self-help books aimed at readers in the corporate world, I have noticed that descriptions of Abraham Maslow's theory of the hierarchy of human needs are often outdated. Typically, 'self-actualisation' is placed in prime position at the pinnacle of the pyramidal diagram that represents this theory. However, towards the end of his life, Maslow realised that self-transcendence was an even greater aspiration.[20] Maslow defined self-actualisation as *finding self-fulfilment and realising one's own potential*. Significantly, he defined self-transcendence as *connecting to something beyond the ego or helping others find self-fulfilment and realise their potential*.

Well before Maslow changed his views, Victor Frankl recognised self-transcendence, not self-actualisation, as the path to a healthy and fulfilling existence.[21] An increasing number of researchers and psychotherapists are now convinced that he was right. Frankl believed it is only by going beyond the self that we find meaning, which he saw as the most basic motivational factor at work in being human. Striving for pleasure, or to gain power, is not sufficient: we need to be dedicated to a task, a cause (religious or otherwise) or another person.[22]

Frankl came to this view, at least in part, through his experiences in a Nazi prison camp during the Holocaust, which claimed his wife and all but one of his Jewish relatives. He noticed that the prisoners who survived the horrific conditions were not necessarily more physically robust than those who succumbed. Rather, they were the ones who were sustained by a sense of meaning and purpose – those who had a reason for living beyond themselves. Subsequently, he wrote:

> It had been overlooked or forgotten [in psychology] that if a person has found the meaning sought for, he is prepared to suffer, to offer sacrifices, even, if need be, to give his life for the

sake of it. Contrariwise, if there is no meaning he is inclined to take his life, and he is prepared to do so even if all his needs, to all appearances, have been satisfied ... The truth is that as the *struggle for survival* has subsided, the question has emerged: *survival for what?* Ever more people today have the means to live, but no meaning to live for.[23]

While Maslow and Frankl both placed great emphasis on self-transcendence – on connecting with something beyond self – their teachings about this were not identical. Maslow's representation of motivational needs as a hierarchic, pyramidal stack has created the impression that self-fulfilment and self-actualisation must be achieved before shifting our attention up a level to helping others (self-transcendence).[24] This interpretation echoes the popular catch-cry invoked to justify selfishness: you must love yourself before you can love others. In contrast, Frankl said that humans 'actualise' themselves (or achieve their potential as human beings) when they are not primarily concerned with themselves but with something – or, even better, someone – other than themselves. In other words, he saw self-transcendence as a key aspect of achieving self-actualisation.

Frankl believed that 'the salvation of man is through love and in love' – that ultimate meaning is supremely expressed in the human capacity to love, not for selfish reasons, but for the sake of the other who is loved. For him this 'other' may be human or divine. He said that a 'religious' person is not satisfied with finding a meaningful task to complete, even when that involves an act of self-giving love. That person will also include the awareness of a transcendent 'task giver', which Frankl described as 'divinity'.[25]

Countless stories could be told of those who, through loving commitment to another, or dedication to a specific calling to serve others, have transcended their own apparent limitations and become a much greater man or woman as a result.

Finding Identity and Meaning

> *The inspiring story of the late king of England, George VI, told so movingly in the multi-award-winning movie The King's Speech, has touched the hearts of millions. Crowned unexpectedly when his brother abdicated, this man rose above a wretchedly disabling stammer to lead his people through the dark days of World War II. Having discovered only recently that I have been battling attention-deficit disorder all my life, I must admit I found myself relating very personally to his struggles with disability. What is more, I also had a troublesome speech defect for which I received months of professional therapy during my college days.*

We are drawn to those who rise above self-indulgent living and commit themselves to greater causes. So often they reflect a depth of character, and even a serenity, that I suspect most human beings long for in their saner moments.

Identity is about us, not me

To many who have been exposed to self-esteem mythology in one form or another for their entire life, the path to meaning advocated by Frankl and others, including myself, may come as a shock – perhaps almost a heresy, comparable to Galileo's championing of the Copernican view that the earth revolved around the sun. A virtual paradigm shift may be required to assimilate it. It does indeed seem paradoxical that to maximise our sense of self – to discover who we really are – we need to reach beyond ourselves.

Identity is about existing as a person, not merely as a human being. It is 'the condition of being oneself … and not another'.[26] Meister Eckhart, a fourteenth-century German mystic, expressed it this way:

> That I am a man,
> this I share with other men.
> That I see and hear and
> that I eat and drink
> is what all animals do likewise.
> But that I am I is only mine

and belongs to me
and to nobody else;
to no other man
not to an angel nor to God
except inasmuch
as I am one with Him.[27]

Eckhart perceived his identity as not only unique but also somehow related to the divine. Sigmund Freud saw identity as shaped by sexuality and experiences of nurture as infants. Alfred Adler, another Viennese psychotherapist, introduced the concept of peer pressure – that our sense of self and how we value ourselves is informed by the way our peers and our siblings respond to us, not simply our own innate perceptions of ourselves. Maslow, as we have seen, depicted us as shaped by a hierarchy of external and inner needs, which control and determine our lives. But for Frankl and many others, paramount to our achieving a healthy sense of identity and our value as a human being is our capacity to interact with others.

The isolated, independent self is a dangerous state of existence. The truth is that we have nothing that we have not received from beyond ourselves, whether by genetic inheritance or as a result of life-long social conditioning (or, as many believe, from God). This applies, one way or another, to every aspect of our conscious and unconscious lives. The current focus on the independent self as the ideal, rather than on the communally integrated individual, is a culturally driven outcome. Cultural drivers are promoting the assumption that focusing on the self in this way is essential to finding one's identity and an intrinsic aspect of the universal nature of being human. This assumption is not true.

Distinguished historian and Christian theologian Dennis Kinlaw believes that the modern and postmodern interest in the self (as distinct from what he calls 'the person'), particularly in the Western world, arose out of ideas introduced long ago by Augustine and

Descartes.²⁸ Augustine, a fourth-century bishop, was convinced that we need to look within even to find God. This 'interiority' was his prime concern. Twelve centuries later, according to Kinlaw, Descartes picked up the concept of interiority but saw it as the means of finding the self:

> Although a theist, [Descartes] did not make the search for God his prime interest. He wanted to find his inner self as a separate and isolated object, the initial building block of epistemological certainty [that is, meaning]. The result was the modern and postmodern search for the self; a search based on the assumption that the isolating of the self might make possible the understanding of the self.²⁹

In contrast, some tribal cultures see identity as derived from our sense of belonging to others. Knowing who I am is discovered by knowing to whom I belong, by being aware of my personhood network: my personhood can only be fully established in neighbourhood. 'Because we are, I am,' they say. I resonate strongly with this view.

While pursuing doctoral coursework in the USA, I took a PhD class in cross-cultural values. At one point the lecturer, a cultural anthropologist, asked the whole class to fill out a standardised form used to assess an individual's hierarchy of values. Two things were a surprise to me. The first was that for all the talk about togetherness, family and community in the USA, the test revealed that the Americans' most intense desire for their children was that they be wealthy, successful and live in a high-status location rather than excelling in terms of civic responsibility, leadership or social engagement. The Americans themselves were shocked by this result.

The second surprise came when it was discovered that two of us were almost off the opposite end of the scale. I was not surprised about myself. As you will be aware by now, I have long been concerned about the lack of communal consciousness in our culture and the overload of radical individualism. The surprise was that the other student who like me was different

> *from the rest appeared to be a typical all-American graduate. He was an outstanding student, an athlete and a natural leader.*
>
> *Later I approached him and asked what made him so different from his peers. He smiled and said, 'My parents were missionaries, and I grew up in an African village where one's identity was deeply rooted in tribal relationships. I guess that has shaped my thinking for the rest of my life.' I might add that he was one of the most socially integrated and likeable people in the whole seminary community.*

Healthy identity is reciprocal. It exists in the context of mutual giving and receiving of our individual uniqueness, not just our possessions. In such a context, we are able freely to offer self-giving love, upon which personal fulfilment depends.[30]

> *In 2011, extraordinary floods and storms ravaged large areas of the state of Queensland in Australia. Many thousands of people were left homeless, or with homes and streets that were severely damaged and filled with stinking mud and debris. It was heart-warming to see how ordinary people came out in droves to assist the victims with the daunting task of cleaning up in the aftermath. Even more remarkable was the flurry of reports in which these volunteers expressed the sense of joy and satisfaction they were experiencing, in the midst of tragedy, as they helped people who were often complete strangers. Those who received this aid also expressed overwhelming joy at being the objects of such care. The gratitude of those who were helped contributed to the sense of purpose and satisfaction of those who reached out to give assistance.*

Countless stories like this could be told about calamities in countries throughout the world. I have included the above example to highlight a paradox that challenges each one of us: *my identity is not all about me, it's about us.* It is about being me in relation to you. My significance is relative rather than absolute. If we attempt to establish our identity by seeking to build our self-esteem without connecting in meaningful ways with others, we are placing the cart before the horse. The call is to experience our 'personhood', our *communal* context of networks and relationships. It is through recognising our personhood, rather than fruitless attempts to commune with our 'authentic self', that we will begin to discover not only our true identity but also a more meaningful and fulfilling life.

12

Exploring the Spiritual Dimension

> Why spend money on what is not bread, and your labor on what does not satisfy? Listen, listen to me, and eat what is good, and you will delight in the richest of fare.[1]

These words were written thousands of years ago by the Jewish prophet Isaiah. He was saying that having sufficient 'bread' to sustain our physical needs is essential, but it is not enough to satisfy the soul and enrich the human spirit.

While contemporary materialism seems to have swept us up in a desire for self-centred pursuits, it has also created a renewed spiritual thirst. As part of our search for meaning, the last few decades have been marked by a return to serious spiritual searching on the one hand and superstition and interest in the paranormal on the other. There seems to be a great longing to connect with a world beyond the physical world we know – to connect with something or someone beyond ourselves.

Cultural historian and social analyst Morris Berman, in a provocative book entitled *The Reenchantment of the World*, describes his

Exploring the Spiritual Dimension

experience of trying to apply a purely objective approach to arriving at truth – and how inadequate he found this approach.[2] He traces the ways in which Western societies since the Enlightenment began placing an increasing emphasis on scientific rationalism and materialism. This process included distancing themselves from the 'irrationalism' of anything that we might term intangible or spiritual in nature. As a result, he says, we have lost something intrinsically important to being fully alive as human beings – an 'enchantment' with which we are striving to reconnect.

More than a hundred years earlier, English poet Matthew Arnold captured beautifully the sadness of such a loss in the following lines from his lyric poem *Dover Beach*:

> The Sea of Faith
> Was once, too, at the full, and round earth's shore
> Lay like the folds of a bright girdle furl'd.
> But now I only hear
> Its melancholy, long, withdrawing roar,
> Retreating, to the breath
> Of the night-wind, down the vast edges drear
> And naked shingles of the world.[3]

The eminent – albeit controversial – Australian historian Professor Manning Clark also wrote eloquently of a loss of the divine. Poignantly, in his classic history of Australia, he entitled one of the chapters *The Kingdom of Nothingness*.[4] He cited Marcus Clarke, Henry Lawson, Adam Lindsay Gordon and Henry Kendall – several of Australia's most famous literary figures of the late nineteenth century – as products of the age of rationalism. He noted that they all expressed lostness, rather than enlightenment, at the death of traditional faith. Each of them also sought analgesic escape in alcohol. At dawn on the day after his most famous volume of poetry was published, Gordon went to the beach and shot himself. Marcus Clarke, writing of his loss of religious faith, described himself as [one who] has stumbled upon the stern rocks ... of Reason, and Practicality and Materialism, and stunned by the fall is no more able to return to the pleasant paths and rest with ease upon the dewy turf but must cling to the rugged and sharp stones around him, lest he fall into the raging sea of despair and utter incredulity that boils and seethes beneath him.[5]

I believe we are still suffering the effects of this loss of faith, or 'enchantment'. The proliferation of self-help books on alternative spiritualities is a clear sign that, no matter how rationalism may sneer, inner doubts about a worldview limited by educated reductionism and objectivity will continue to gnaw at us. The market exploits this yearning through books and other media with offerings ranging from the sublime to the ridiculous, sometimes reducing spirituality to little more than self-indulgent sensuality.

With the approach of millennial celebrations at the end of the twentieth century, there was much talk of a new age of unprecedented, unlimited prosperity, and even a new age of cultural understanding of global justice. For many people, God did not come into the picture in this brave new world. Why did we need God? We were now the captains of Spaceship Earth as well as our own destinies. Many dismissed God as a figment of the imagination, a placebo, a crutch for the weak, rather than a meaningful help. Then came the horrors of 11 September 2001. In New York, the Twin Towers were obliterated and thousands died. Suddenly, there was a renewed interest in the concept of sin and evil. How can we go on believing in the intrinsic goodness of the human race when such an unthinkable event happens?

Not only that, but aggressive fundamentalism in various religious forms – Islamic, Christian and Jewish – was kickstarted into new life. Since then, we have had to learn to live with fear, which is something prosperity alone can never relieve. Rather than the new millennium leading us to a self-assured and holistic culture, it has reignited ancient traditions and fears and raised again questions concerning the meaning of life and death. Many even in the business world are now returning to religious consciousness, although not necessarily to its traditional forms.

Subjectivity and spirituality

As human beings, we are incorrigibly subjective. Anthropologists tell us that a unique element of being human is our capacity to project subjective meaning and values into what we observe. As a result, things we see and create may become symbols that are meaningful to us without necessarily having any intrinsic meaning.

Some things have an *intrinsic value*, of course – an inherent, objective value. For example, a house has intrinsic value, irrespective of its market price or sentimental value to us, because by its very nature (being a house) it provides us with shelter. However, when we bring a value from outside and attribute it to something, we give it a subjective *extrinsic value*. For example, a mother may treasure a child's drawing as though it were a genuine work of art, while others would see it as merely a scrap of paper and consign it to the waste bin.

Some would argue that our intrinsic value as human beings lies in the fact that we are an amazing and complex organism with the capacity to think, socialise and love. A problem with this secular point of view is that, irrespective of our complexity and capabilities, it ultimately relegates humans to being meaningless products of the same unfeeling forces that rust iron and ripen corn. Proponents of this view may go so far as to suggest that, given we are the most environmentally destructive creatures on the planet, it would be best for the rest of the biosphere if we were not here at all. The alternative viewpoint would argue that we have intrinsic value because we are made in the image of God and are the object of a Divine purpose.[6] Many of the bitter debates concerning abortion and euthanasia arise out of the differences between these perspectives.

Whatever our worldview, the fact remains that we do project or insert values which are expressed in symbols and rituals. Because there is such a subjective element in this process, we are in frequent conflict over what we treasure and see as significant. A symbol of hope to one person provokes subjective despair in another. The sign of the cross to a Christian may speak of life-giving love, whereas to a follower of Islam with the knowledge of the Crusades, it may speak of violence, conquest and bloodshed. One person's meat is another person's poison.

It is normal for human beings to internalise what is happening, to reflect upon it and interpret the outside world in terms of inner feelings and past experiences. It is a manifestation of the self-consciousness that is an essential property of being human. Viktor Frankl refers to this as 'the transcendent unconscious', which for him means 'no more or less than that man has always stood in an intentional relation to transcendence, even if only on an unconscious level'.[7]

A unique experience of ourselves in relation to the invisible and mysterious aspects of the world is inescapable for each of us, no matter how scientific and rational we may seek to be. Similarly, although traditional religion tells us that the truth is 'out there', independent of what we think about it, all religious dogma is nevertheless an interpretation of the inner life of those who write and teach it. As the physical world is only recognisable through our physical senses, the values of perceived truth, love and meaning are only observable from within as we reflect upon them.

It is our subjective reflection that enables us to be creative and makes it possible for individuals to respond to similar situations in very different ways. Poetry, music and theatre are saturated with 'self-conscious' or subjective reflections evoked by the natural world but interpreted within each individual or collective culture. Contemplating the night sky, especially in a region unpolluted by city lights, often inspires deep inner experiences. For the ancient Jewish songwriter

David, who would stargaze as he guarded his father's sheep, the stars sang of Divine significance:

> The heavens declare the glory of God;
> > the skies proclaim the work of his hands.
>
> Day after day they pour forth speech;
> > night after night they display knowledge.
>
> They have no speech, they use no words;
> > no sound is heard from them.
>
> Yet their voice goes out into all the earth,
> > their words to the ends of the world.

Elsewhere he writes:

> When I consider your heavens,
> > the work of your fingers,
>
> the moon and the stars,
> > which you have set in place,
>
> what is mankind that you are mindful of them,
> > human beings that you care for them?[8]

His subjective response to the universe, the vastness and beauty of the night sky, was to say: 'What am I? What is humanity? How extraordinary we must be that we are on the personal agenda of the Divine.'

Well-known Australian broadcaster and writer Phillip Adams, an avowed atheist, writes about the sense of the 'numinous' he experiences:

> To feel it, go outside tonight and stare up at the stars. The sense of awe and wonderment and dread that floods your soul — or should, if you haven't been taking pills — is the numinous. Which has inspired not only our curiosity but our greatest art, buildings, poetry, music, philosophy and, yes, religion.[9]

In his book *Unseen Footprints*, Christian communicator Sheridan Voysey also writes about those moments when we sense that something (or perhaps Someone) bigger than us has been encountered.[10]

At ten years of age I read *The Mysterious Universe* by British astrophysicist Sir James Jeans. No doubt I was unable at that age to understand most of the intellectual theory, but it impacted me for life. Jeans was attempting to explain, to the non-scientific mind, Einstein's theory of relativity and the speed of light. My child's mind was transfixed by the possibility that some of the stars we now view ceased to exist eons ago. The sky always engulfed me in a deep sense of mystery and wonder. I still find myself breathing more deeply when alone under the night's canopy.

I was brought up in a Methodist manse and strongly influenced by the Christian faith of my parents. By the end of my school years, however, my faith was becoming overwhelmed by unanswered questions promoted by secular rationalism. It had worn so thin that, secretly, there were many days I doubted it all. I had what I perceived to be authentic spiritual moments, followed by bleak meaningless days. I think that, as a rather serious kid, I perhaps experienced what the mystics called 'the dark night of the soul' a little earlier than most. At teachers' college, the last tenuous tones of Divine music were briefly silenced completely.

> One winter's night, I stood out on a veranda looking at the stars, very conscious of my aloneness. On this occasion, the stars did not lead me to God as they do now. They led me to despair. French existentialists Sartre and Camus had become my literary companions, a path that was leading me towards meaninglessness. The myriad stars and the immensity of the heavens led, not to wonderment at the mystery of human existence, as they had done for David, but to a sense of utter insignificance.

An earlier experience during my final year at high school also affected me deeply, although I doubt it had a lasting impact on any of my classmates. One day in assembly our English teacher, a remarkable and gifted man I feel privileged to have known, quoted a few lines by the Australian poet Adam Lindsay Gordon:

> Life is mostly froth and bubble
> Two things stand like stone
> Kindness in another's trouble
> Courage in your own.[11]

The charisma of my teacher, his voice, his conviction and his passion made these seemingly trite lines of homespun wisdom seem crucially important to me. It was as though God had stopped everything for that moment so that I could ponder them. I have never forgotten that experience and I still feel what I felt then – a call to personal courage and determination, matched by kindness offered to others less fortunate. Once I had resolved some of the inner turmoil of my search for self and meaning, it was to become a guiding principle for my life.

In my early twenties, soon after coming out of my time as a virtual closet atheist, I had another intensely spiritual experience. It is almost impossible for me to describe this in words that would make sense to you. All I can say is that it left me in no doubt whatsoever that there is a Divine Other. It also left me with a deep assurance, also beyond rational explanation, that I had an ultimate value: I had a mission to fulfil and my life had purpose. In the many years that have gone by since then, I have had doubts about all kinds of things – just about everything, it might be fairer to say – but the certainty I felt about the reality of the Divine in that experience long ago has never left me.

Remarkable subjective experiences happen to most people from time to time. You may well have your own stories to tell. Even those skilled in the art of scientific enquiry are not excluded. I remember reading a book entitled *The Tao of Physics* by Fritjof Capra.[12] Here was a man with an outstanding scientific mind who came to the conclusion that physics, the study of the physical universe, was not simply about objective measurements. While sitting and watching the ocean with its endless rhythms of ebb and flow, he had experienced a 'mystical revelation'. Meaning, organic unity and spirituality became interwoven with his scientific knowledge as he reacted uniquely to his visual observation of nature.

Biologist Charles Birch, the first scientist to win the Templeton Prize for his contribution to philosophy and religious thought, wrote in his book *On Purpose*:

> I am not a materialist. The prime reason is that I have had experiences which materialism cannot explain. Secondly I know too much about matter from modern physics to be a materialist ... Because I find materialism incredible [unbelievable], I look for an alternative view that will be true to my profoundest feelings and to the understanding I find from modern science.[13]

Some years ago an exhibition of religious art was held at the Victorian Arts Centre in Melbourne. It featured Arthur Boyd's celebrated painting of the Jewish prophet Moses leading his people to the land they had been promised by God. I was pleasantly surprised when the exhibition drew record attendances because I saw this as an expression of secular Australia's deeper, genuine religious and spiritual inquiry.

Similarly, I and many others were surprised at the huge popularity and lengthy success of Caroline Jones's ABC TV program *Search for Meaning*. Over its eight-year run, hundreds of Australian men and women told of their experiences. Subsequently her book *An Authentic Life: Finding Meaning and Spirituality in Everyday Life* became a bestseller. I have also noted that a program on ABC Radio National entitled *The Spirit of Things*, which began in 1998, is still going to air. I see this as another challenge to the assumption that materialism has silenced the quest for the transcendent among the vastly secular Australian culture.

It seems that the prophecies of secular psychologists, sociologists and anthropologists, that a scientific society would eclipse religion, have proved to be at least premature. Although earlier Freudian analysis of the human psyche saw any religious inclination as neurosis, later pioneers in the field of psychology – Jung, Adler, Maslow, Frankl and many subsequent leaders in the field – have embraced the spiritual elements of humanness.

Psychiatrist and historian Eugene Taylor has written extensively about the renewed interest in alternative spiritualities that emerged during the countercultural revolution of the 1960s.[14] He also documents two previous major shifts from materialism to spirituality throughout the history of the Western world, and he sees this cycling as an expression of the mysterious self-consciousness that belongs to being human. It is as though the stench of self-serving greed, materialism and war has driven cultures towards deeper religious consciousness – as though a search for deeper meaning makes sense when such pursuits fail to satisfy a society. My hope is that we will again tire of the corrosive effects of materialism and individualism and seek the qualities that truly sustain humanity.

Despite the many confusing trails that may be laid before us in this information age, we remain not only *free* to search for spiritual truth but also *predisposed* to search for it. The danger is that we will allow the media and assorted gurus to home in and capitalise on this innate human desire, rather than taking control and seriously exploring it ourselves. We need to ensure that a healthy, humble sense of mystery, a yearning for meaning and an attitude of goodwill to others is not supplanted or confounded by rationalistic secularism, loveless religious fundamentalism or unexamined forms of psychic experimentation.

13

The Most Seductive Myth of All

In his classic book *The Brothers Karamazov*, Dostoevsky says through the Grand Inquisitor, 'The everlasting wish of the human race is to find someone to worship.' Self-esteem mythology neatly solves that problem for us by elevating the self to god-like status. What could possibly be a greater boost to the sagging self-esteem than hearing the seductive words: 'All power and wisdom reside within you. Just listen to your inner voice, the authentic you, the god within you, and all will be well.' Through such inducements, the self is enticed into a role that belongs more appropriately to a god-like entity than a human being.

The I-am-God myth

The idea that 'I am God/Goddess' is a logical extension of the me-focused attitudes that are engendered by the myth of self-esteem. It is tantamount to saying, 'I am the most wonderful and important being in the universe and entitled to unceasing adoration and praise.' It makes *me* all powerful and all-knowing and all-wise. I can be, do and have anything I desire, and if something goes wrong it cannot possibly be my fault. This way of thinking, which is surely the ulimate in narcissitic grandiosity, is not unique to the self-esteem movement. It is part of a large area of intersection between the myth of self-esteem and New Age thinking.

The philosophy of the New Age movement became popularised during the countercultural revolution of the 1960s, coinciding with a renewed interest in the spiritualities of primitive cultures such as paganism, with its belief in multiple gods or goddesses, and pantheism. The movement offered a potpourri of alternative spiritualities, which adherents could dip into as they wished, or incorporate into whatever formal religion they chose to follow.

A wide range of alternative spiritualities now huddle under the huge umbrella of the New Age movement, whose roots Eugene Taylor traces back through 300 years of emerging interest.[1] Aspects of this eclectic movement are often referred to as 'pop psychology', especially by its detractors. It is true that this apparently spiritual movement is also a profoundly psychological one, stressing the alteration of consciousness, the integration of mind and body, and the connection between physical and mental health. As part of this process, spirituality has been redefined.

Interest in New Age spiritualities is well and truly alive in the present day. For example, *Encounter*, an ABC national radio program about spirituality, devoted an entire episode to the topic of paganism in 2011. In the UK, the website of the BBC includes a calendar of pagan events. Every year people from all over the country gather in Nottingham for a pagan festival. And in the USA, a reviewer has described the 2009 film *Avatar* as an 'apologia for pantheism', explaining why he believes pantheism has been 'Hollywood's religion of choice for a generation now'.[2]

Of the many spiritualities on offer, pantheism is the most closely allied to the I-am-God myth. Pantheism is the belief that nature and God are identical. God is everything that exists, and in everything that exists. This 'God' is not a divine entity separate from ourselves.

Rather, according to the pantheistic view, we are part of the totality of nature that is God. Therefore, each person can say 'I am God' and seek God within him or herself. A dedication to 'the sacred child in all of us' offered by the publisher of a children's book is just one example of the ways in which pantheistic thinking has permeated our culture.[3]

If there is a primary mantra of the self-esteem movement, it may well be summed up in directives such as *listen to your heart, follow your heart, trust your heart*. All are expressions of the idea that the self is the ultimate source of wisdom. This has been a central theme in many daytime TV shows, including *The Oprah Winfrey Show*. Although Oprah may be well-intentioned, her pronouncements about spirituality over the years have been decidedly confused, and confusing. For example, the following are among the quotes she has offered as maxims for life:

> Nothing is at last sacred
> But the integrity of your own mind. *Ralph Waldo Emerson*
>
> Just trust yourself,
> Then you will know how to live. *Goethe*
>
> Follow your instincts.
> That's where true wisdom manifests itself. *Oprah*[4]

Preaching a form of spirituality that is 'all about me', she says: 'It isn't until you come to a spiritual understanding of who you are – not necessarily a religious feeling, but deep down, the spirit within – that you can begin to take control.'[5]

Through such statements, I have no doubt that Oprah has been instrumental in promoting the I-am-God myth. The same can be said for Dr Phil, with his exhortations to connect with your unerring 'authentic self'. He not only preaches the I-am-God myth but, at times, deals so authoritatively with those who appear on his shows

The Most Seductive Myth of All

that I get the impression he also believes it fervently himself.

I find it strange that many people who would regard it as reasonable to reject the notion of the Pope's infallibility now so readily believe in their own. In a book entitled *Your Sacred Self* – written by another self-styled guru, Wayne Dyer – I found some astonishing assertions. For example: 'You are sacred, and in order to know it you must transcend the old belief system you've adopted ... You are a divine being called to know your sacred self by mastering the keys to higher awareness.' He also writes:

> The physical changes that will take place in the world will happen automatically, just as they will in your body when you shift to your sacred self. This is inevitable. The ego fades in the brilliance of the divine light. You find you are behaving in more peaceful and loving ways. So too will this take place on a global level.[6]

Another guru, who now describes herself as an executive wealth coach, is Dr Judy Moss. Listing levels of consciousness, she refers to the highest as 'the super-conscious mind', which 'remains pure and accurate at all times and is uninfluenced by anything or anyone and therefore entirely reliable = your 'true self'.[7] She also claims that self-guidance or intuition is 'your ultimate teacher and your sure-fire insurance policy for success'. Thus her message, like Dr Phil's, is that the *real* you is omniscient, omnipotent and infallible. In other words, you are God!

In the complex world of human longing and losing, these and many other self-help gurus have emerged with their faith messages and magic solutions, which are on even shakier ground than the dubious seductions of the old Elmer Gantry-style tent religion (revisited in Steve Martin's movie *Leap of Faith*).

Ralph Waldo Emerson pre-empted the I-am-God myth in his influential essay on self-reliance. In the nineteenth century, he taught that the ultimate source of truth resides within oneself and presented fidelity to one's inner promptings as the basis for authentic life.[8]

In the contemporary Western world, this view has been reinforced by the fact that ordinary people, having reached a high degree of comfort, security and independence, assume a 'new sense of power over their own fate, the belief in unbounded possibilities of improving their own lot'.[9]

Accompanying this, in both the secular and the religious domains, has been a growing emphasis on fulfilling your destiny. To many, this means the unrestricted pursuit of personal ambition and the free expression of one's individual desires. But others have a monumentally different view. For them, fulfilling their destiny means responding to what they perceive as an external calling to serve others.

The inspirational movie *Invictus*, which portrays events in the life of the anti-apartheid campaigner Nelson Mandela, features the words of William Ernest Henley:

> It matters not how strait the gate,
> How charged with punishments the scroll,
> I am the master of my fate:
> I am the captain of my soul.[10]

How sad it is that with these heroic-sounding words the movie unwittingly teaches the I-am-God myth. It is also promoting the whatever-you-want-to-be myth by taking the rare example of an ordinary person who rises to great heights against all odds, and presenting it as if it is a universal principle and an attainable destiny for anyone.

In contrast, at a public presentation during a visit to Sydney, Mandela himself ascribed his commitment to human rights to the influence of his Methodist Church roots. He said that during his many years imprisoned in the now notorious Robben Island Prison, he only once, through physical disability, missed the worship services provided there. Surely that is quite incongruous with the notion that Mandela saw himself as the god-like master of his fate and captain of his soul, as presented in *Invictus*. It is clear that he looked to a power higher than himself for his strength and inspiration.

Finding our way

If we dismiss the I-am-God option as a myth, what is left for us? We can believe in nothing at all beyond ourselves and the material world – an option chosen by some – or we can consider one of the many other spiritualities now on offer.

When we look below the surface, it becomes apparent that many of the spiritual options now available to us are primarily market driven. It has been said, 'When people don't believe in God, they don't believe in nothing, they believe in anything.'[11] People living in a materialistic – and increasingly secular – society, who see themselves as free from the superstition of the church, tend to become the creators of new superstitions that offer less certain paths to salvation.

I see it as no coincidence that in those parts of the world where material prosperity has been attained, a smorgasbord of spiritualities has been embraced by intellectuals, counsellors, human rights activists, corporations and, overwhelmingly, by the popular culture and the arts. While most have rejected the views of traditional religion, they embrace pre-modern, non-materialistic spirituality almost without critical analysis.[12] Surprisingly, many well-educated people seem willing to adopt an alternative spirituality with much less questioning and discernment than they would apply to making choices about secular issues.

Once when I was travelling in Southern France, I picked up a hitchhiking Brit. He was a young graduate student from Brighton who was on holidays. He told me he had converted to Buddhism although our conversation left me doubting whether he had ever been a convert to anything but materialism. His hometown, he informed me, was a gathering place for young 'Buddhist neo-pagan' seekers and practitioners, apparently oblivious to the incongruity of this label. Who would have prophesied that Brighton would be a hotbed of alternative religion at the dawn of the twenty-first century?

In my suburb, spirituality now has nothing to do with human solidarity, a Divine Other or the thoughtful management of God-given resources for the sake of those who have less. For some, spirituality may be doing a yoga class so that they can feel less stressed and be re-energised to go back into the dog-eat-dog world. Melbourne's *Herald Sun*, in its 'body+soul' section, has provided inserts that define spirituality in terms of sensuality. In Britain, I watched a 'world expert on angels' telling a bemused journalist on BBC TV that faith in 'Asphaltia', a neo-pagan goddess of highways, would guarantee a car park at the supermarket every time!

We have travelled from the arid desert of rationalism to a bewildering jungle of competing spiritualities. Sadly, you can die in a jungle as easily as in a desert. I often encounter a deep longing for spiritual truth and meaning, struggling for survival amidst the tangle of alternatives on offer:

> *Some years ago I accepted an invitation to give a talk about 'Gods Squad spirituality' to a group I later discovered had beliefs that were very different from mine. There were Christians who objected to my accepting an invitation from these 'evil New Agers'. The talk went ahead, and the response from the mixed audience of young adults and elderly people was explosive – so much so that I was invited to stay for the next session to be presented by their best psychic medium.*
>
> *Although I sat myself in what I thought was an inconspicuous place, the psychic immediately singled me out. She said that someone 'on the other side', dressed in leathers with a beard and ponytail was trying to make contact with me, and she did her best to get me to put a name to this person. When I told her honestly that I knew a large number of people fitting that description who had 'passed over', the performance fell flat. Her next attempt to communicate with the other side was no more successful. She said she was not doing well that night, perhaps because they were all shaken up by what I had said.*
>
> *The psychic then told us that she once had a terrible skin disease that nothing would fix. One day she picked up a Bible and read the account of*

Jesus healing a person with a skin disease. She said that Jesus 'told' her to wash her hands under the tap, which she did. She was convinced that Jesus was responsible for the healing that ensued.

At supper afterward, the group asked me to say more about the Bible and the spiritual issues I had raised. I happily obliged.

I realised that these people were not enemies of traditional faith, they were fellow travellers genuinely seeking spiritual truth. The older ones especially had lost someone dear to them and, feeling isolated and afraid of what was to come, were looking for answers – for hope in an afterlife and reconnection with their loved ones.

New Age alternatives – which include spiritualism, with its focus on contacting the dead, as well as throwbacks to paganism, pantheism and Wicca – are not the only options we have for acknowledging a sense of mystery. They are not the only ways of reaching beyond the restrictions of scientific rationalism to find a vibrant human identity.

Time after time, throughout our history, those who have led us to what is claimed to be a higher consciousness and a new understanding of our humanity are those who call on the wisdom of past mystics and very ancient religious traditions: Christianity, Islam, Buddhism, Judaism and Hinduism.[13] Wisdom is also to be found in ancient tribal cultures, such as those of the Native Americans and the indigenous people of Australia. Recently a young Canadian Native American, reflecting on our Western disdain for the past and obsession with the future, said to me: 'In our culture we say, "We walk backwards into the future".'

It is true that the great religions of the world have produced some bad outcomes, particularly when married to politics: war, terrorism, conflict and corruption. We cannot hide from that. It is equally true, however, that when such religious expression is faithful to the founders' principles, it produces spiritually attuned carers for humanity. such as William Wilberforce (abolition of slavery), William and Catherine Booth (founders of the Salvation Army), Mahatma Gandhi and the present-day Dalai Lama. These are but a few among the many self-transcendent champions of mercy, human dignity and human rights whose wellsprings of compassion are religious in origin.

As I have explored the lives of such true champions of human freedom, I have found that their focus is not on themselves, their achievements or the public acclaim. Instead I have found a serenity of spirit, a healthy sense of self and a detachment from the manipulations of money and power, all rooted in faith and love. Many of these champions have also chosen to isolate or distance themselves, to a greater or lesser extent, from the manipulative influences that distort our sense of self and create in us a narcissistic need to impress the world around us.

I am not for a moment suggesting that the great saints of the past or the present are without their inner struggles and their outer foibles. Nor am I suggesting that those without religious faith are unable to make worthwhile contributions to society. That is demonstrably untrue. Nevertheless, in those whose singular willingness to live self-sacrificially is an expression of their religious devotion, there is often a serenity born of separation from concerns about image and success.

As well as the exceptional people who reach celebrity status even though they do not seek it, there are many people of genuine religious faith who quietly contribute to the wellbeing of others, unseen and uncelebrated. Many of my generation count our caring grandparents of another era among these unsung heroes. Consistent with this, a recent large academic study of people in Germany found that religious people tended to give higher priority to altruistic and family goals than non believers, and lower priority to success goals.[14] Interestingly, it was also found that people who became more religious over time showed long-term gains in life satisfaction, while those who became less religious showed long-term losses.[15]

Even secular commentators at times recognise the innate needs of the human soul, and that there is a place for healthy forms of faith in the process of finding meaning and community. Dick Gross, an outspoken atheist, wrote in his newspaper column *Godless Gross*: 'My view is that the church is very adept at dealing with suffering through support systems, the post mortal consolation and its underlying narrative of social justice.'[16] Clive Hamilton notes that many who follow a religious path become incorporated into faith communities 'where they can, for a time at least, immerse themselves in a social environment that is welcoming, caring, joyous and devoted to a higher purpose. This is a rare experience nowadays, but it fulfils an essential human need – one that television, shopping malls and political parties cannot meet.'[17]

My chosen path

Many years ago I made a life-transforming choice to become a follower of Jesus and embrace authentic Christianity. I do not mean the travesty of Christianity that throughout history has found expression in war, hatred, bigotry, extreme conservatism, intolerance and sexual predation. Nor the kind that comfortably indulges itself while others suffer, or cons the public into giving money in return for religious favours. That is not authentic Christianity as embodied and taught by Jesus Christ, the One who was prepared to suffer an excruciating death to affirm the reality of his message and mission of Divine love for the whole of humanity.[18]

Lamentably, the popular media tends towards the controversial, the bizarre and the fringe when portraying the search for spiritual truth. There are very few thoughtful or provocative media presentations about the human struggle for identity, direction and Divine love, or the teachings of Jesus for that matter, though the market is plainly there. Rather, we are served up a diet of chat-show guests with wacky but attention-grabbing ideas about spirituality. At the same time, any failings of those who profess to be Christians are presented with great relish. These include not only the truly scandalous incidents involving paedophile priests and philandering evangelists, but also fictional portrayals of vacuous, simpering vicars or sexually repressed Christian do-gooders and kill-joys.

Within the Christian community itself, regrettably, there are some who reduce their faith to the self-focused life as promoted by self-esteem mythology. They are often attracted to churches that teach a 'prosperity gospel'. This trendy version of Christianity declares that God's blessings are often materialistic and that they are there for the asking for all those who have sufficient faith to claim them. This is the sexy God of pop-Christianity and TV's God channels. Some see this prosperity variant as a sign of a less repressive and liberating faith. I see it as a diversion from the true inclusiveness and liberation that is part of authentic Christianity and other great world religions.

If you are feeling motivated to explore the spiritual dimension of your life, may I encourage you to include an examination of the person and teachings of Jesus Christ.[19] Many millions of people throughout the world, including myself, revere him as the One who is the very embodiment of God's love for humanity, and gladly devote their lives to serving others as an expression of their devotion to him.

Perhaps you have been turned off such an exploration by the Christians you know. A few years ago, a Sydney-based Christian media organisation distributed posters with the message 'Don't let Christians put you off Jesus'.[20] I agree wholeheartedly. It saddens me deeply when I see Jesus being misrepresented, not only by those who do not know or appreciate him but also by those who profess to be his followers. We Christians can fail dismally when it comes to demonstrating the loving compassion and other gracious 'fruit' that are expressions of the Spirit of Jesus Christ – 'love, joy, peace, forbearance, kindness, goodness, faithfulness, gentleness and self-control.'[21]

It is possible to visit some churches that are so 'what's in it for me'-focused that they are barely distinguishable from the surrounding culture. In contrast, others may be so hide-bound by their political structures and traditions that their ability to reflect the true nature of

Jesus is severely hampered. These are not accurate representations of the Christian movement established by Jesus, which arose from a vibrant, life-transforming, faith-based counterculture. So compelling was its message of hope that, in its first 300 years, it spread like a wildfire throughout the entire known world, despite intense and deadly opposition from the establishment.[22] It is still thriving.

In your spiritual searching, you will need to be discerning if you are to discover the truth about the deep issues of faith, meaning and identity.

14

Self-Esteem and Self-Surrender: The Ultimate Paradox

I was in my early twenties when I read an article in a Melbourne daily newspaper about a search for truly happy people. I realise now, of course, that the methodology of such studies is often questionable, and I cannot vouch for its claims. Nevertheless, I remember being amazed at how few people would admit to great happiness. The two who did were a nun and an elderly Salvation Army officer, both of whom were committed to serving others as an expression of their deep religious conviction.

Many famous people we respect and admire as people of magnificent intellectual creativity and attractive humanity are also people of self-transcendence, committed to serving others – people like St Francis of Assisi, Mother Teresa, Mary McKillop, Desmond Tutu and Mahatma Ghandi. All were people who espoused willing surrender and acknowledged a meaning and spiritual inspiration greater than themselves. A prayer attributed to St Francis was quoted by Mother Teresa when she addressed the UN in 1985. It offers us a deeply felt expression of such self-surrender:

Self-Esteem and Self-Surrender: The Ultimate Paradox

> Lord, make me a channel of thy peace.
> That where there is hatred I may bring love,
> That where there is wrong, I may bring the spirit of forgiveness,
> That where there is discord, I may bring harmony,
> That where there is error I may bring truth,
> That where there is doubt I may bring faith,
> That where there is despair I may bring hope,
> That where there are shadows I may bring light,
> That where there is sadness I may bring joy.
> Lord, grant that I may seek rather to comfort than to be comforted,
> To understand than to be understood,
> To love than to be loved.
> For it is by forgetting self that one finds.
> It is by forgiving that one is forgiven,
> It is by dying that one awakens to eternal life.[1]

There is a marked difference between this attitude and the viewpoint expressed in the well-known song 'My Way', which emerged as a Frank Sinatra hit in the 1960s. This song has since been recorded by many artists, and it is still a popular choice at funerals, even the funerals of those who have a 'religious' service. I suspect that it is often chosen because it seems to celebrate a life that has been lived with integrity: it may be seen as a fitting tribute to someone who has remained true to themselves by making life choices without yielding to pressure from peers or the world around them. However, if you google 'My Way' and take a closer look at the lyrics, you will see that there is more to it than that. The person depicted not only boasts that they have been able to chart their course through life without leaning on other people but also proudly declares their independence from God. They have not been someone who 'kneels', they say. They have been completely self-reliant and self-sufficient.

The contrasting worldviews expressed in the two lyrical works described above epitomise a choice that confronts each one of us. I can carry on doing it *my way* as taught by the myth of self-esteem: I can be my own 'god' and devote my life to exalting myself. Or I can choose to acknowledge a power greater than myself and willingly surrender to living *his way*,[2] that is, God's way.

The belief that we are the 'masters of our fate' and 'captains of our soul' is embedded deeply in the psyche of the postmodern Western world. From this point of view, to think otherwise is to diminish our sense of self – to risk doing irreparable damage to the precious self-esteem that we see as essential to finding success and satisfaction. But here is the ultimate paradox. The experience of countless people who have followed the path of willing surrender to a higher power is this. By surrendering themselves they have truly found themselves – and the sense of purpose and fulfilment they have been seeking all their lives. This, in part, is what Jesus meant when he said, 'Whoever tries to keep their life will lose it, and whoever loses their life will preserve it.'[3]

The paradox of finding self by surrendering self has often found expression in poetry, which is surely an appropriate vehicle for an experience so profound and so subjective that it is almost beyond words. Hymnology of all major world religions abounds in such expressions. The following hymn from the Christian tradition is a good example:

> Make me a captive, Lord,
> and then I shall be free;
> force me to render up my sword
> and I shall conqueror be.
> I sink in life's alarms
> when by myself I stand;
> imprison me within thine arms
> and strong shall be my hand.

Self-Esteem and Self-Surrender: The Ultimate Paradox

> My will is not my own
> till thou hast made it thine;
> if it would reach a monarch's throne
> it must its crown resign;
> I only stand unbent
> amid the clashing strife
> when on thy bosom I have leant
> and found in thee my life.[4]

Of course, when it comes to surrendering ourselves, it is critically important that the one to whom we surrender is worthy of our trust. For many, the horrendous results of so-called holy wars and modern jihad would make surrender to any cause other than self-interest seem like a very risky proposition. Adding to this wariness, we have the madness of demagogues such as Hitler, and the cult leader Jim Jones who led more than 900 men, women and children in his commune to death by mass suicide. Whether we are committing ourselves to citizenship of a nation, a romantic or business relationship, or to a higher power, mindless surrender without a moral and relational framework is never healthy.

As one who long ago surrendered his life to God as revealed in Jesus, I can say that this has been the wisest, most fruitful and most fulfilling decision of my life. I have found where I truly belong. I agree with Augustine of Hippo, who some 1600 years ago summed up relationship with God this way: 'You made us for yourself, and our hearts find no peace until they rest in you'.[5]

Many postmodern people regard traditional religion as locked into doctrines of self-denial. From my faith perspective, however, I can assure you that Christianity does not call for a suppression or denial of everything that makes us the unique human beings we are. Theologian Robert Hillman has addressed this topic in a very helpful way. Describing those who choose the Christian path of surrendering wholeheartedly to God, he writes:

> Ultimately, being true to one's real self means ... serving [Jesus Christ] in loving, free obedience and then serving others in his name, even to the point of being prepared to lay down one's life for them. But it does *not* mean having low self-esteem and a poor self-image or being a 'doormat'. In humble gratitude, the Christian stands at his or her full height as he or she is aware of being, in Christ, a unique, infinitely loved and gifted personality. Thus the hallmark of the healthy self is humility, but not self denigration ... there should be a sober, realistic acknowledgment of strengths and abilities.[6]

Hillman goes on to say that those who surrender themselves in this healthy way will have confidence, with Divine help, to assert themselves when appropriate. But, in true humility, they may also at times choose graciously to lay aside what may be considered their rights in order to fulfil a higher purpose. The following description of Jesus illustrates exquisitely both self-surrender and true humility:

> He had equal status with God but didn't think so much of himself that he had to cling to the advantages of that status no matter what ... When the time came, he set aside the privileges of deity and took on the status of a slave, became *human*! Having become human, he stayed human. It was an incredibly humbling process. He didn't claim special privileges. Instead, he lived a selfless, obedient life and then died a selfless, obedient death – and the worst kind of death at that – a crucifixion.[7]

For anyone who accepts this as truth, as I do, the fact that the Divine chose to become human and live among us as the 'God-man' Jesus, offering us personal relationship with him, underscores our profound individual significance to him.

Self-surrender is not simply a means of finding inner serenity, as some of my neo-Buddhist friends would suggest. It does not wrap the individual in a feel-good cocoon isolated from social connection

Self-Esteem and Self-Surrender: The Ultimate Paradox

with others. It incorporates concern for human justice and caring about and connecting with our neighbour. In its noblest form, it is about unconditional love.

Here is a timeless story in which the surrender of self becomes a pivotal event. It is the story of a man born in Egypt more than 3000 years ago – a story that has become part of the tradition of three great world religions: Judaism, Christianity and Islam.[8]

He emerged out of obscurity as the child of an enslaved racial minority. While still a baby, he was separated from his parents as part of the oppression they suffered. Although adopted by a significant member of the dominant Egyptian culture, he nevertheless was deeply affected by the apparent insignificance of his ethnic heritage. As an adult, incensed by the maltreatment of one of his people, he murdered an Egyptian overseer and had to flee into the surrounding wilderness to escape the wrath of the most powerful, wealthy, innovative nation of his time. From such unlikely beginnings, he went on to become a central hero in the story of the Jewish people, eventually securing their release from Egypt and leading them to freedom – and to a new land where they became a great nation.

This man is now honoured as a prophet by three of the world's most influential religions. He has also been an ongoing inspiration to well-known leaders of the twentieth century in their efforts to effect social transformation, and he continues to impact our culture. The two greatest speeches given by Martin Luther King Jr in his struggle against racial segregation in the USA are loaded with allusions to this man's story, as are black gospel and folk music. Yet he was a man who suffered from an overwhelming sense of what we would now call low self-esteem. His genius was to rise above his circumstances and limitations, not by finding strength from within himself, but by reaching beyond himself.

As a fugitive living in the wilderness at the edge of the desert, his life became that of a simple herdsman. As time went by, his former life of privilege was left far behind. At that point in his life, he could never have imagined the role that awaited him. But before he could become the liberator of the Jewish people, he had to find out who he was. Paradoxically, this turned out to be a question, not of his own identity but rather of the identity of God. The wilderness became not only his place of concealment but also the place where he discovered his destiny.

One evening, the story goes, our hero, whose name is Moses, while returning from his daily chores, observes from a distance a strange phenomenon. It is a bush that appears to be burning but is not being consumed by the fire.

A voice from the bush tells him that his destiny is to liberate his people from the horrendous tyranny of Egypt. 'No way!', he thinks. The Egyptian empire is one of the most powerful in the ancient world. It is highly civilised and organised. It has conquered powerful nations. His own Jewish community, in contrast, is little more than a loose confederation of subsistence herdsmen. Our 'hero' goes into a self-esteem meltdown. Why him of all people? He has no status, no wealth or influence, no military might to call upon. Apart from that, he is wanted for murder back in Egypt!

Painfully aware of his insignificance, Moses tells the voice from the burning bush that he is quite unsuited to a confrontation with Pharaoh, the world's most powerful man. He reminds the voice that although he was adopted by Pharaoh's daughter, his family lineage was that of a despised Jew whose mother belonged to the slave class.

In other words, he is saying, 'Who am I to address the great Pharaoh? I'm a nobody. I just look after livestock.' He might well have added that the latter task suited a person of low self-esteem such as himself. At least the animals in his herd would recognise him as superior to themselves, even if nobody else did.

The voice from the bush identifies itself. The name is that of the Holy One, Yahweh, the great I AM, which means something like 'I am who I am. I always have been and always will be. I am the eternal I am'.[9] *What an extraordinary sense of identity this name implies!*

The voice tells Moses words to this effect: 'You will go to Pharaoh not simply on the basis of your own authority. You are to tell him that I AM has sent you.' This is the voice of One who suffers no identity insecurity – I

AM has nothing to prove. At this point, if Moses is willing to receive it even hesitantly, he is being granted what anthropologists call 'ascribed status'. Because the One who represents the ultimate is sending him, there will be an authority that is above and beyond anything Moses could call upon from any other source.[10]

As a fugitive from the law, Moses is hardly equipped to make a moral demand upon the Pharaoh – to confront him and say 'Let my people go!', as he is instructed to do. But the voice reminds him that the authority he needs to do so (which will become integrated into Moses' own essential identity) comes from beyond himself. Moses again protests that he is particularly unsuited to the task because he has a communication problem – he has trouble stringing his words together, as is often the case for people who are shy or lacking self-confidence.

At this point the voice from the bush, with great forbearance, reminds him that his tongue has been created by the One to whom he is speaking: the great I AM. This is the One who is the ultimate, benevolent, all powerful source of Moses' capacity to talk. What is more, he is also the source of the moral compulsion and commitment to justice that will become so much part of Moses that it will carry him back to Egypt and into the throne room of the mighty Pharaoh to plead for his people.

And so the story continues, telling how Moses, with the new-found strength and sense of identity and purpose that flowed from his surrendering of self to the good purposes of the great I AM, went on to fulfil his destiny in remarkable ways.

For most of us, it is unlikely that our destiny lies in becoming a great hero whose name will be remembered throughout history. But like Moses, we too can move beyond the barrenness and limitations of focusing on ourselves and depending on our own finite resources. By surrendering ourselves to the all-wise, all-loving God by whose empowerment Moses was transformed, we too can discover a new sense of purpose, a new concern for others and the fulfilment that comes from knowing we are in the place where we belong.

Acknowledgements

Coming up with dissenting and novel ideas has never been difficult for me. But maintaining the discipline to stay focussed on one issue over the many years it takes to bring a book to completion – that is a different matter. This book would never have been published if it were not for three significant people.

The book had its origin in an address entitled 'Feeling good about doing bad', which I presented to thousands of young people at the 2004 Greenbelt Christian arts festival in the UK. By the end of the twentieth century I had become increasingly concerned about the influence of the so-called self-esteem movement. I was convinced it would be destructive and that it was psychologically unsound. At Greenbelt, my unconventional views about self-esteem did not go down well with some of the 'youth counsellers' in the audience, but the positive response from the young people was overwhelming.

Soon after I returned from the UK, I received an email from Dai Hughes, a Welshman who had found faith and redirection for his life through an earlier book I had written. He had been transformed from a self-centred entrepreneur and highly successful creative realtor into a social activist. He was emailing to ask if I was still pursuing transformational writing. And he was offering me retreat at his parents' villa in the south of France as well as generous financial support so that I could escape other distractions that winter and write another book. An initial draft encompassing the whole spread of ideas in this book was completed during my three months there. You would not be reading this if it were not for Dai and his family's sacrificial gift.

However, with the many distractions in my life, creative and otherwise, the essential next steps – the ordering of the content and complex research – may never have been completed were it not for the input of two other people. First, I want to acknowledge the steadfast support of my far-more-ordered and administratively responsible wife Glena. Her constant disciplinary pressure to bring this book to completion was essential, as was her encouragement to persevere when the going got tough. I did not always take kindly to this, of course, but I now see it as a gift – a crucial balance to my tendency to become bored, distracted or disheartened and just move on before finishing a project.

Second, some decades ago, Glena and I became friends with Coral Chamberlain, an astute biomedical researcher whose previous experience in scientific writing, supervising doctoral students and editing books made her another ideal 'disciplinarian', as well as a professional evaluator of my writing. The many, many hours we spent reassessing the text, via one form of electronic communication or another, and our shared commitment to the task enabled that initial draft created in the south of France to be reordered into a logical and coherent manuscript for publication. While the fundamental ideas may have come from me, an immense amount of research, application and justification for the arguments of this book came from years of tireless commitment on Coral's part. She has been an amazing editor and co-writer – *par excellence*.

No words can express the depth of my gratitude to Dai, Glena and Coral. Thank you for believing in me, keeping me focussed and rearranging my initial spontaneous outpourings of disparate ideas into a coherent argument with passion. You are all very dear to me.

I also want to express my gratitude to Sheridan Voysey, Dave Waters, Daniela Witschel, Elaine Abrahams, Judi Parker and Carol Jesson, who read drafts along the way and provided insightful comments and encouragement; and Hugh Mackay for kindly granting permission to quote from his works. Acorn Press Ltd are deserving of my special thanks, particularly, Paul Arnott, Gina Denholm and Kristin Argall, who have fulfilled their roles with skill and grace. Undeterred by my often controversial views and the fact that this book did not fit neatly into any of the usual genres, they have courageously and generously embraced it.

Acknowledgements

Above all, I am grateful to God who, fortunately, did not shape us all in the same mould but has allowed for the dissenting mind and chaotic creativity.

Notes

1. Self-Esteem, Self-Respect or Self-Obsession?

1 **Clive Hamilton,** *The Freedom Paradox: Towards a Post-Secular Ethics*, Allen & Unwin, Sydney, 2011, pp. 15–17. Hamilton says, 'There is nothing inherently virtuous about the *good life* – except in so far as one believes that cultivating our talents is intrinsically worthwhile.' In contrast, Hugh Mackay describes the *good life* as a virtuous life in which we treat others as we ourselves would wish to be treated; see Hugh Mackay, *The Good Life*, Macmillan, Sydney, 2013.

2 **Hugh Mackay,** 'So much love, but sadly it's the wrong kind', *The Sydney Morning Herald (SMH)*, 16 December 2006, http://www.smh.com.au/news/opinion/so-much-love-but-sadly-its-the-wrong-kind/2006/12/15/1166162317625.html?page=fullpage. Used by permission.

3 **When I use the term** 'pop psychologist' I am referring to either unqualified people who dabble in psychology, or psychologists who exploit opportunities for public exposure in order to achieve celebrity. I am not referring to the vast majority of psychologists in clinical practice, who are highly trained and fully accredited. They generally have the best interests of each patient at heart and offer genuine assistance to those struggling with life issues.

4 **Factiva search** of all UK newspapers between 1980 and 2001; cited in Frank Furedi, 'Inaugural lecture: Making people feel good about themselves. British social policy and the construction of the problem of self-esteem', 24 January 2003, http://www.frankfuredi.com/articles2.shtml.

5 **Historical information** in the following paragraphs is from Carol Craig, 'A short history of self-esteem', 2006, see under 'Confidence' at http://www.centreforconfidence.co.uk/pp/positive-psychology.php; Roy F. Baumeister et al., 'Does high self-esteem cause better performance, interpersonal success, happiness, or healthier lifestyles?' *Psychological Science in the Public Interest*, vol. 4, no. 1, May 2003, pp. 1–44, http://www.

psychologicalscience.org/journals/pspi/pdf/pspi411.pdf; Martin E. P. Seligman, *The Optimistic Child: A Proven Program to Safeguard Children against Depression and Build Lifelong Resilience*, Houghton Mifflin, Boston, 2007.

6 **The first of Nathaniel Branden's books** on self-esteem was *The Psychology of Self-Esteem: A New Concept of Man's Psychological Nature*, Nash, Los Angeles, 1969; another, still widely read, is *The Six Pillars of Self-Esteem*, Bantam, New York, 1994.

7 **See** *Macquarie Dictionary Online*, 2014.

8 **In 2006,** journalist Michael Lallo listed what he believed to be the seven biggest myths of the self-help movement. Lallo's list includes slick adages such as *you can achieve anything, trust your gut instinct, it's not your fault*. See Michael Lallo, 'Busted: the seven biggest self-help myths', *The Age*, 6 November 2006. While there is some overlap between his list and the self-esteem myths I describe, there are also important differences.

9 **For example,** Jean M. Twenge & W. Keith Campbell, *The Narcissism Epidemic: Living in the Age of Entitlement*, Free Press, New York, 2009. An early voice raised against the growing trend of self-absorption was Christopher Lasch, author of *The Culture of Narcissism: American Life in an Age of Diminishing Expectations*, Norton, New York, 1979, and *The Minimal Self: Psychic Survival in Troubled Times*, Norton, New York, 1984.

10 **Martin Luther King Jr** pointed to a growing tendency in Western civilisation to confuse 'means' and 'ends' in *Strength to Love*, Collins-World, Cleveland, 1963.

Chapter 2. The Be-Whatever-You-Want-To-Be Myth

1 **From 'When you wish upon a star',** a song by Ned Washington and Leigh Harline ©1940 Bourne Co. Used by permission. This song was an early expression of the yearning that underlies the be-whatever-you-want-to-be myth.

2 **Clive Hamilton,** 'The disappointment of liberalism and the quest for inner freedom', Discussion Paper No. 70, The Australia Institute, Canberra, 2004, p. v.

Notes

3   **For all its weaknesses,** the Trade Union Movement in Australia and the UK has fought for, and achieved, a liveable minimum wage in these countries.
4   **Gregg Easterbrook,** *The Progress Paradox: How Life Gets Better While People Feel Worse*, Random House, New York, 2004, p. 258. Easterbrook writes of chance encounter that made him realise that the money he spent on take-away lunches each week represented the equivalent of a whole week's net pay for a minimum wage receptionist working nearby (p. 262).
5   **On 3 October 2011,** in an episode of ABC TV's *Four Corners* entitled 'Poor Kids', it was claimed that 'the gap between rich and poor is now wider than at any time since the Second World War'. This episode included a moving documentary in which some of the estimated 3.5 million children who are growing up poor in the UK spoke of their experiences; see 'Poor Kids', a documentary directed by Jezza Neumann, True Vision, London, 2011, http://truevisiontv.com/films/details/63/poor-kids. It was also noted that more than 46 million people in the USA (15% of the population) were living in poverty in 2010.
6   **The be-whatever-you-want-to-be myth,** already well established in the USA, received a further boost when Barack Obama was elected as President in 2009. Here was apparent evidence that in America anyone, even an urban black kid, could rise to the most exalted position in the land (although Obama was no ordinary black urban kid, of course). In a culture that wants to dampen down racial urban conflict this is a very useful concept to sell, placing the blame back on the urban poor for their failure to get a job or rise out of poverty. But what if Obama had lost the next election?

Chapter 3. The You-Must-Feel-Good-Look-Good Myth

1   **The latter slogan** is from an advertisement for Marriot Hotels.
2   **Based on Easterbrook,** *The Progress Paradox*, p. xiii.
3   **Life expectancy in the USA** is now about 76 years for males, 81 years for females and even higher in Australia and the UK. Modern medicine

has not only extended life expectancy but also quality of life for most.
4 **Martin Seligman,** 'Forum on Depression', *Life Matters*, ABC Radio National, 16 September 2002 (recorded 1994); see also Seligman, *The Optimistic Child*, p. 42.
5 **Paul Brand & Phillip Yancey,** *The Gift of Pain: Why We Hurt and What We Can Do about It*, Zondervan, Grand Rapids, 1997.
6 **Described in the** Yalata Aboriginal Community's *Maralinga: The Anangu Story*, Allen & Unwin, Sydney, 2009.
7 **Richard Rohr,** *Breathing Underwater: Spirituality and the Twelve Steps*, Saint Anthony Messenger, Cincinnati, 2011. Rohr is the founder of the Center for Action and Contemplation.
8 **Caroline West,** 'Work four hours, then rest', *SMH*, 4 August 2009.
9 **Hugh Mackay,** 'The pursuit of happiness will make you miserable', Festival of Dangerous Ideas, Sydney Opera House, 2–3 October 2010, http://play.sydneyoperahouse.com/index.php/media/978-hugh-mackay-the-pursuit-of-happiness-will-make-you-miserable.html.
10 **Mackay,** *SMH*, 2006. Used by permission.
11 **Ibid.**
12 **Hugh Mackay,** 'Life is about compromise', *The Age*, 27 June 2005. Used by permission. Mackay refers to this attitude as 'the utopia complex' in *The Good Life*, 2013.
13 **Viktor E. Frankl,** *Man's Search for Meaning: The Classic Tribute to Hope from the Holocaust*, Rider, London, 2004, p.116. First published in German in 1946.
14 **Robert Browning Hamilton** in William R. Bowlin (ed.), *A Book of Personal Poems*, Albert Whitman & Co., Chicago, 1936, p. 101; popularised in a song by Barry Mann performed by folk-rock singer Barry McGuire in the 1970s.
15 **Seligman,** *The Optimistic Child*, pp. 44–5.
16 **Luther King Jr,** *Strength to Love*, p. 31. No doubt his statement applies equally to women.
17 **Based on** the British Association of Aesthetic Cosmetic Surgeons' 2012 Annual Audit, 28 January 2013, http://baaps.org.uk/

about-us/press-releases/1558-britons-raise-a-few-eyebrows; the American Society of Plastic Surgeons' 2012 Annual Statistics Report, 6 February 2013, http://www.cossurgery.com.au/2013/02/20/non-surgical-treatments-drive-cosmetic-surgery-growth.

18 **Comment by** the President of the Cosmetic Physicians Society of Australasia, 16 February 2012, http://www.costhetics.com.au/news/australians-outspend-us-on-cosmetic-procedures.

19 **Mindy Laube,** 'Groomed for success', *SMH*, 4 September 2009.

20 **A bill banning child beauty pageants** was recently passed by the French Senate, 18 September 2013, http://www.dailymail.co.uk/news/article-2424462/France-bans-girls-beauty-contests-bid-stop-hyper-sexualisation-children.html. It was based on a parliamentary report entitled *Against Hyper-Sexualization: A New Fight For Equality*, which also called for the banning of sales of child-sized adult clothing such as padded bras and high heels; also see http://www.minorcon.org/padded_bras.html, September, 2006.

21 **From UK Department of Health,** *Review of the Regulation of Cosmetic Intervention*, April 2013, p. 12, https://www.gov.uk/government/uploads/system/uploads/attachment_data/file/192028/Review_of_the_Regulation_of_Cosmetic_Interventions.pdf. In a recent Australia-wide survey of more than 14,000 young peoples aged 15–19 years, about 30% indicated that body image was a major concern for them; see Mission Australia Youth Survey 2013, https://www.missionaustralia.com.au/research-page/cat_view/37-research/41-young-people.

22 **Maxine Frith,** 'Children as young as 11 are unhappy with their bodies', *The Independent*, 2 April 2005, http://www.independent.co.uk/life-style/health-and-families/health-news/children-as-young-as-11-are-unhappy-with-their-bodies-530788.html. The unrealistic physical proportions of toys such as Action Man and Barbie dolls were also condemned.

23 **Martin Lindstrom** with Patricia B. Seybold, *BrandChild: Remarkable Insights into Today's Global Kids and Their Relationships with Brands*, Kogan Page, London, 2004, p. 77.

24 **Diana Loomans,** *The Lovables in the Kingdom of Self-Esteem*, H. J. Kramer/Starseed, Tiburon, 1991. Illustrated by Kim Howard.

Chapter 4. The Boosting-Self-Esteem-Brings-Happiness Myth

1 **Seligman,** *The Optimistic Child*, pp. 34–5.
2 **Baumeister,** *Psychological Science in the Public Interest*.
3 **In these studies,** assessments of happiness and self-esteem were subjective, that is, based on opinions expressed by each participant. Self-esteem assessment procedures, including the widely used Rosenberg method, are reviewed in Nicholas Emler, 'Self-esteem: the costs and causes of low self-worth', Joseph Rowntree Foundation, York, 2001, pp. 7–12, http://www.jrf.org.uk/sites/files/jrf/1859352510.pdf.
4 **Po Bronson,** 'How not to talk to your kids. The inverse power of praise', *New York Magazine*, 11 February 2007, http://nymag.com/news/features/27840.
5 **Our perception of happiness** (or wellbeing, the term preferred by psychologists) is highly subjective and influenced by many life factors, making it very difficult to measure just how happy someone is. Differing assessment methods are used and the results will be influenced by complex factors, including the range of issues selected for assessment, the design of questionnaires and the bias and/or competence of the assessors. Richard Eckersley and Robert Cummings claim to have produced the world's first Personal Wellbeing Index; see Richard Eckersley, *Well & Good: Morality, Meaning and Happiness*, 2nd edn, Text Publishing, Melbourne, 2005, p. 84, http://richardeckersley.com.au/main/page_books_books_page_1.html. The factors they considered were: standard of living, health, achievements in life, personal relationships, safety, community connections and future security.
6 **Martin Seligman,** *The 7.30 Report*, ABC TV, 7 December 2009, http://www.abc.net.au/7.30/content/2009/s2764376.htm.
7 **Easterbrook,** *The Progress Paradox*, p. xvi.

8 **Bruce Headey et al.**, 'Long-running German panel survey shows that personal and economic choices, not just genes, matter for happiness', *Proceedings of the National Academy of Sciences*, vol. 107, no. 42, Oct. 2010, pp. 17922–26.
9 **Henry Samuel**, 'Millionaire gives away fortune that made him miserable', *The Telegraph*, 8 February 2010.
10 See http://www.beyondblue.org.au; beyondblue is an Australia-wide, independent organisation dedicated to raising community awareness about depression and acceptance of those who suffer this condition.
11 **Easterbrook,** *The Progress Paradox*, p. xvi.
12 **Clive Hamilton & Richard Denniss,** *Affluenza: When Too Much Is Never Enough*, Allen & Unwin, Sydney, 2005, p. 112.
13 **Hamilton,** 'The disappointment of liberalism and the quest for inner freedom', p. v.
14 **Hamilton,** *The Freedom Paradox*, 2011, pp. 3, 305.
15 **Martin E. P. Seligman,** *Learned Optimism: How to Change Your Mind and Your Life*, William Heinemann, Sydney, 2011, pp. 10–13, 282–90; see also Seligman, *The Optimistic Child*, chapter 5.
16 **Seligman,** *The Optimistic Child*, p. 37.
17 **Seligman,** *The 7.30 Report*.
18 **Allan V. Horwitz,** 'How an age of anxiety became an age of depression', *Milbank Quarterly*, vol. 88, no. 1, Mar. 2010, pp. 112–38.
19 **Martin E. P. Seligman,** *Flourish: A Revolutionary New Understanding of Happiness and Well-Being*, William Heinemann, Sydney, 2011, p. 79.
20 **World Health Organization,** 'The global burden of disease: 2004 update', World Health Organization, Geneva, 2008, http://www.who.int/healthinfo/global_burden_disease/2004_report_update/en.
21 See   http://www.mentalhealth.org.uk/content/assets/PDF/publications/fundamental_facts_2007.pdf.
22 See   http://www.blackdoginstitute.org.au/docs/Factsandfiguresaboutmentalhealthandmooddisorders.pdf.
23 **'National College Health Assessment:** reference group report', American College Health Association, Baltimore, 2004, as described

by Richard Kadison, 'Getting an edge – use of stimulants and antidepressants in college', *New England Journal of Medicine*, vol. 353, no. 11, September 2005, pp. 1089–1091, http://www.nejm.org/doi/full/10.1056/NEJMp058047.

24 **American Psychological Association,** 'School-based program teaches skills that stave off depression', 27 October 2003, http://www.apa.org/research/action/school.aspx.

25 **Jean M. Twenge,** *Generation Me: Why Today's Young Americans Are More Confident, Assertive, Entitled – and More Miserable Than Ever Before*, Free Press, New York, 2006, p. 107. Twenge and her team analysed data from 40,000 college students and 12,000 children who completed anxiety measures between 1952 and 1993 in the USA. They found that the average college student in the 1990s was more anxious than 71% of college students in the 1970s. The trend in children was even more marked.

26 **Jean M. Twenge et al.,** 'Birth cohort increases in psychopathology among young Americans, 1938–2007: A cross-temporal meta-analysis of the MMPI', *Clinical Psychology Review*, vol. 30, no. 2, Mar. 2010, pp.145–54; reported by Martha Irvine, 'Study: Youth now have more mental health issues', *Boston Globe*, 11 January 2010.

27 **Seligman,** *The 7.30 Report*, 2009.

28 **Eckersley,** *Well & Good*, p. 4. He also lists autonomy, competence, purpose, direction, balance and identity as factors that contribute to a satisfying and meaningful life.

29 **For help dealing with suicidal thoughts,** you can phone Lifeline (13 11 14) or the Salvo Care Line (1300 36 36 22) in Australia or a similar organisation in your country. The study described was carried out by social researcher Trevor Chambers and reported in part by Tim Costello in 'The "youth suicide" myth', *The Age*, 17 October 2000. The projection for a boy aged 15 years in 1998 was based on suicide rates for that year, ignoring any escalation of rates beyond that and by projecting male suicide rates into the future (as for published divorce statistics); the risk of this boy's dying in his teens was relatively low. Indeed a new finding of this study was that the actual suicide rate was consistently

much lower for 15–19-year olds than for 20–39-year olds. Death-by-suicide rates for females remained stable and relatively low in all age groups over the study period. See also http://www.abs.gov.au/ausstats/abs@.nsf/Lookup/by%20Subject/1370.0~2010~Chapter~Sui cide%20%284.5.4%29. The number of deaths per suicide attempt is much higher for males than for females because males tend to use more decisive, violent methods.

30 **Nadja Reilly,** 'A primer on childhood and adolescent depression', July 2008. Dr Reilly is an expert in child and family mental health at Massachusetts School of Professional Psychology.
31 **Eckersley,** *Well & Good*, chapter 9.
32 **Ibid.,** p. 179.
33 **Luke 12:15,** *The Holy Bible*.
34 **This is my summation** of Easterbrook's analysis. Easterbrook, *The Progress Paradox*; based on pp. xviii, 85, 106–7, 137.
35 **Richard Eckersley,** 'Casualties of change, the predicament of youth in Australia: An analysis of the social and psychological problems faced by young people in Australia', Australian Government Publishing Service for Commission for the Future, Canberra, 1988, http://www.richardeckersley.com.au/attachments/CFF_Casualties_1988.pdf. Many of the issues highlighted in this report remain pertinent today: see Douglas Rushkoff, *Present Shock: When Everything Happens Now*, Current, New York, 2013; Sherry Turkle, *Alone Together: Why We Expect More from Technology and Less from Each Other*, Basic Books, New York, 2011.
36 **Daniel Sieberg,** 'The Digital Diet: How to break free of your smart phone and other gadgets', *Washington Post*, 28 May 2011, and *The Digital Diet: The 4-Step Plan to Break Your Tech Addiction and Regain Balance in Your Life*, Three Rivers, New York, 2011.
37 **Seligman,** *Learned Optimism*, pp. 284–6; Seligman, *The Optimistic Child*, p. 42.
38 **Richard Eckersley,** 'Youth and the challenge to change: Bringing youth, science and society together in the new millennium', Australia's Commission for the Future, Carlton South VIC, 1992, http://www.

richardeckersley.com.au/attachments/CFF_Challenge_1992.pdf.
39 **Seligman,** *Learned Optimism,* pp. 10–13, 282–290.
40 **Seligman,** *Flourish,* p. 79.
41 **Seligman,** *The Optimistic Child,* p. 42.

Chapter 5. The All-About-Me Myth

1 **Clive Hamilton,** *The Freedom Paradox,* p. 6.
2 **Richard Eckersley,** 'Never better – or getting worse? The health and wellbeing of young Australians', Australia 21 Ltd, Canberra, 2008, http://www.richardeckersley.com.au/attachments/A21_youth_health__wellbeing.pdf.
3 **From an essay** *On Liberty* by John Stuart Mill, first published in 1859; discussed in Hamilton, *The Freedom Paradox,* chapter 2.
4 **Hamilton,** *The Freedom Paradox,* pp. 28–9.
5 **Steve Biddulph,** an internationally recognised parenting expert and author, has described escalating sexualisation of the young as 'society's cancer' (*SMH,* 26 February 2013, http://www.smh.com.au/federal-politics/contributors/sexualisation-of-the-young-is-becoming-societys-cancer-20130225-2f1y4.html).
6 **Anthropologist Robert B. Edgerton,** in his book *Sick Societies: Challenging the Myth of Primitive Harmony* (Free Press, New York, 1992), comments that all societies for the whole of recorded history have some elements of oppression and dysfunction. In some cases these are minor, in others they can threaten an entire culture's survival. It is also true that throughout history some social patterns have proven to be healthy and effective across space and time and cultures. Some elements of the ritual process of transition from childhood to adulthood found commonly across many cultures are currently of great interest to social scientists and spiritual practitioners because they appear to address some of the serious problems associated with the existing generation gap.
7 **I see the social disintegration** of Australia's indigenous youth as almost inevitable following decades of appalling government policies of

forced removal of children, now known as the 'stolen generation', with disruption of parent–teenager relationships and tribal customs associated with transition to adulthood.
8 **Young people raised** in a strongly Confucian worldview are deeply imbued with reverence for ancestors and profound respect for parents and teachers. I discovered during graduate studies that adult students from this culture evidenced a genuine respect for the professors that was entirely lacking in their American and Australian counterparts, including myself.
9 **George C. Boeree**, 'Viktor Frankl. 1905–1997', 2006, http://webspace.ship.edu/cgboer/frankl.html.
10 **Robert Van de Weyer** (compiler), *On Living Simply: The Golden Voice of John Chrysostom*, Liguori/Triumph, Liguori, 1996, p. 16.
11 *ABC News*, 25 July 2013, http://www.abc.net.au/news/2013-07-25/town-mayor-arrested-over-bangladesh-factory-collapse/4844074, AFP.
12 **When another well-known** Australian philanthropist and businessman Dick Smith urged wealthy compatriots to join him in giving generously to charity, he reportedly said: 'If they were giving their money away, it's amazing what happens with karma. The right things would happen for them' (see 'Tycoon Dick blasts Australia's "appalling and greedy" super wealthy', *SMH*, 21 December 2010). Had experience taught this canny entrepreneur that his peers would not be moved by an appeal based purely on compassion for the homeless who were to benefit? While I have some problems with the karma concept generally, overall I am very impressed with Dick Smith's maverick and disturbing way of challenging his own philanthropic culture.
13 **An old Swedish proverb** quoted by Phillip C. McGraw, *Self Matters: Creating Your Life from the Inside Out*, Simon & Schuster Source, New York, 2001, p. 165.
14 **Ecclesiastes 4:9–10**, *The Holy Bible*.
15 **The pastor had graduated** in psychology and his wife was a former teacher. They were strongly influenced by the theories of British psychologist Dr Frank Lake. See Lake's *Clinical Theology: A Theological and*

Psychiatric Basis to Clinical Pastoral Care, Emeth Press, Lexington, 2005.
16 **For more about the notion** of personhood see Dennis F. Kinlaw, *Let's Start with Jesus: A New Way of Doing Theology*, Zondervan, Grand Rapids, 2005; quotation from pp. 81–2.
17 **Luke 9:25,** *The Holy Bible*.
18 **Proverbs 30:8–9,** *The Holy Bible*.
19 **Seligman,** *Learned Optimism*, pp. 282–6. He says 'our epidemic of depression is a creature of the maximal self', p. 284; also Martin E. P. Seligman, 'Why is there so much depression today? The waxing of the individual and the waning of the commons,' in Rick Ingram (ed.), *Contemporary Psychological Approaches to Depression: Theory, Research, and Treatment*, Plenum, New York, 1990.
20 **Eckersley,** *Well & Good*, p. 4.
21 **From the 1923 song** 'Nobody knows you when you're down and out' by Jimmie Cox, first popularised by Bessie Smith and more recently by Eric Clapton.
22 **Robert D. Putnam,** *Bowling Alone: The Collapse and Revival of American Community*, Simon & Schuster, New York, 2000.
23 **Amy Corderoy,** 'Money not the key to happiness', *SMH*, 10 July 2010, reporting a study by Ed Diener et al., *Journal of Personality and Social Psychology*, vol. 99, no. 1, Jul. 2010, pp. 52–61.

Chapter 6. The Never-My-Fault Myth

1 **From a poem** by Alexander Pope (1688–1744).
2 **Romans 12:3,** *The Holy Bible*.
3 **Seligman,** 'Forum on Depression'.
4 **Adapted from John Irvine,** 'Praising Children', *9am with David and Kim*, TV Channel 10, 30 May 2007; see also John Irvine, *Who'd Be a Parent? The Manual that Should Have Come with the Kids!*, Pan Macmillan, Sydney, 1998.
5 **Paul Tough,** 'What if the secret to success is failure?' *New York Times Magazine*, Education Issue, 14 September 2011, http://query.nytimes.

com/search/sitesearch/#/paul+tough.
6 **Eckersley comments** that survey results showing a high level of moral doubt and ambivalence among Australians are hardly surprising given that the mass media make virtues of what were once regarded as vices while neglecting the traditional virtues. There is thus a lack of cultural reinforcement to live out the values that matter to a society; Richard Eckersley, 'Values and visions – youth and the failure of modern Western culture', *Youth Studies Australia*, vol. 14, no. 1, 1995, p. 16, http://www.richardeckersley.com.au/attachments/YSA_values_1995.pdf.
7 **Seligman,** 'Forum on Depression'.
8 **Peter Fraser,** letter to the editor, *SMH*, 1 September 2009. At the inquest in 2011, despite evidence from dozens of students, teachers and medical experts, wildly conflicting accounts led to an 'inconclusive' finding.
9 **See Genesis 2:1–13,** *The Holy Bible*. The serpent, according to some wit, didn't have a leg to stand on!
10 **Georgina Robinson,** 'Irate cyclist attacks bus driver', *SMH*, 26 October 2009.
11 **Seligman,** 'Forum on Depression'. TV psychologist Phillip McGraw also cautions against becoming prisoners of the past in *Self Matters*, 2001. Individuals who genuinely need to revisit their past can do so under professional supervision. Psychotherapists are trained to guide this process without being judgemental or apportioning blame. Many psychotherapists, while taking into account their patients' past experiences, now use approaches that help the individual face the reality of their present situation and develop strategies for dealing with it. This seems decidedly more helpful than earlier approaches that tended to entrap people in a victim mentality.
12 **Lallo,** *The Age*, 2006.
13 **Tiger Woods' friend,** American billionaire Donald Trump, is quoted as saying about the damaged marriage, 'I would recommend Tiger just call it a bad experience, say bye-bye, go out and be a wonderful playboy and win tournaments and have a good life' (Neil Gardner, 'Tiger Woods

should become a playboy', says Donald Trump', *Times Online* [London], 19 February 2010).
14 **Lallo,** *The Age,* 2006.
15 **Bellinda Kontominas,** 'Hoyts sued over fall on "hazardous" stairs', *SMH,* 5 November 2009; 'Commuter claims £1.5m after slipping on "killer" petal outside florist', *London Evening Standard,* 17 July 2007.
16 **As a result,** two years later I had the privilege of addressing a full hearing of the UN Human Rights Commission in Geneva on behalf of prisoners of conscience.
17 **Amitai Etzioni,** *The Spirit of Community: Rights, Responsibilities, and the Communitarian Agenda,* Crown, New York, 1993; Robert N. Bellah et al., *Habits of the Heart: Individualism and Commitment in American Life,* University of California Press, Berkeley, 2007.
18 **Barbara Ehrenreich,** *Smile or Die: How Positive Thinking Fooled America and the World,* Granta, London, 2009, pp. 187–9.
19 **Steve Fishman,** 'Burning down his house', *New York Magazine,* 30 November 2008.

Chapter 7. Gurus of the Myth of Self-Esteem

1 **Mackay,** *SMH,* 2006. Used by permission.
2 **Unless otherwise indicated,** information in this section comes from http://www.oprah.com/pressroom/Oprah-Winfreys-Official-Biography.
3 **Mary Corey,** 'Self-esteem arrives as talk show issue', *Baltimore Sun,* 16 June 1990.
4 **Reported in Emler,** 'Self-esteem', p. 64.
5 **Robyn Okrant** has written entertainingly about her struggles to achieve her 'best life' by spending a year living according to the wisdom of Oprah Winfrey and following every piece of advice she offered her through her TV show, magazine and website, in *Living Oprah: My One-Year Experiment to Walk the Walk of the Queen of Talk,* Center Street, New York, 2010; the author was interviewed by Nick Gatlin, *The Sun-Herald,* 25 April 2010.

6 **See** http://www.oprah.com/omagazine/What-Oprah-Knows-for-Sure-About-Finding-Success. Martin Luther King Jr is often quoted by self-esteem gurus, but even a cursory reading of his classic book *Strength to Love* shows that his worldview is quite contrary to self-esteem mythology and Oprah's focus on personal success.
7 **See** http://www.great-inspirational-quotes.com/best-friend-quotes.html.
8 **See** http://www.oprah.com/oprahshow/A-Lifesaving-Oprah-Show-Message-Video.
9 **Weston Kosova**, 'Why health advice on "Oprah" could make you sick', *Newsweek*, 29 May 2009, updated 22 November 2011, http://www.newsweek.com/why-health-advice-oprah-could-make-you-sick-80201; Brad Newsome, 'Is Oprah bad for your health?' *SMH*, 9 December 2010.
10 **Patricia Sellers**, 'Oprah's next act', *Fortune*, 18 October 2010.
11 **Phillip McGraw**, 'Dr. Phil defends intentions with Britney Spears', TV interview on TODAY, 1 February 2008, http://www.today.com/id/22901694#.UzKEv4URdL9.
12 **McGraw**, *Self Matters*. The quotations that follow are, in order, from pp. 248, 286, 41.
13 **Ibid.**, pp. 285–6.
14 **Ibid.**, pp. 19–20.
15 **Ibid.**, pp. 282–4.
16 **While I do accept** that divorce may be necessary in extreme circumstances, for example, where there is violence or mental cruelty, I believe the present focus on self contributes unnecessarily to divorce statistics. Adding to this is a decline in adherence to religious faith, which previously would have encouraged many to work at relationships, favouring reconciliation through mutual repentance and forgiveness rather than quitting.
17 **Steve Salerno**, *SHAM: How the Gurus of the Self-Help Movement Make Us Helpless*, revised edn, Nicholas Brealey, London, 2006, p. 8.
18 **Lallo**, *The Age*, 2006.
19 **Robert H. Schuller**, *Self-Esteem, the New Reformation*, Word, Waco,

1982. Another example is *Power Thoughts: Achieve Your True Potential through Power Thinking*, HarperCollins, New York, 1993. He says, 'If you can dream it, you can do it'.

20 **Steve Arman,** Simon Bird & Malcolm Wilkinson, *Reformation and Rebellion: 1465–1750*, Heinemann, Oxford, 2002.

21 **John 10:10,** *The Holy Bible.* Jesus said: 'I have come that they may have life, and have it to the full [abundantly]'. Elsewhere the Bible makes it clear that the abundant life Jesus offers comes as a gracious gift. It cannot be earned, nor is it related to material status.

22 **In more extreme versions** of this deviation, some preachers maintain that the true believers are Jesus the King's 'kids' and therefore deserve all that King's kids should have – the very best of food, clothing, transport, etc. Some even claim that the wealth of their society will be redirected to the true believers.

23 **Trinity Broadcasting Network Europe,** *Weapons of Power*, 1 March 2005.

24 **Loomans,** *The Lovables in the Kingdom of Self-Esteem*, 1991.

25 **Social psychologist** Professor Joanne Wood and her team have shown that repeating an affirmation intended to boost confidence – in this case 'I am lovable' – does in fact leave some people with low self-esteem feeling worse; Joanne V. Wood et al., 'Positive self-statements: Power for some, peril for others', *Psychological Science*, vol. 20, no. 7, Jul. 2009, p. 860–6.

26 **For several decades,** my wife and I have had enriching relationships with indigenous Australians. The tendency of indigenous people to look at the ground while being addressed is often assumed to indicate that their self-esteem is low. But in tribal terms, it is a matter of respect, protocol and established relationship: I must *earn* the right to stare into your eyes. Furthermore, in light of the seminar presenter's assertions, it seems somewhat bizarre that prisoners and those regarded as socially inferior within our Western culture can find themselves in trouble for arrogance if they dare to stare out their 'superiors'.

27 **Mackay,** *SMH*, 2006. Used by permission.

Chapter 8. A Rising Tide of Dissent

1 **Craig,** 'A short history of self-esteem', 2006. Craig, who is based in the UK, describes the work of academics Roy Baumeister (a former supporter of the self-esteem movement), Nicholas Emler, Martin Seligman, Jennifer Crocker and Jean Twenge.
2 **Ibid.;** Emler, 'Self-esteem'; Baumeister, *Psychological Science in the Public Interest*; Twenge, *Generation Me*.
3 **Lauren Slater,** 'The trouble with self-esteem', *The New York Times*, 3 February 2002, http://www.nytimes.com/2002/02/03/magazine/03ESTEEM.html. This article in the popular press was pivotal in stimulating debate. Although open to criticism by those seeking academic rigour, it does contain seeds of truths worthy of serious consideration. In response to Slater, Vasconcellos attempted to justify his position; see John Vasconcellos et al., 'In defense of self-esteem', http://www.self-esteem-nase.org/amember/newsarticles/InDefenseofSelf-Esteem.pdf (no date). A major flaw in his article is the unfounded assumption that it is only 'healthy, authentic self-esteem' that results from interventions implemented to boost self-esteem, ignoring the possibility that decidedly unhelpful practices may have been introduced. I was able to trace only one of the studies cited by Senator Vasconcellos to support his case, a study by Michele Borbain that was not representative of the feel-good approaches that are widely used and now under censure.
4 **These include authors** cited throughout this book; also John P. Hewitt, *The Myth of Self-Esteem: Finding Happiness and Solving Problems in America*, Contemporary Social Issues Series, St Martin's Press, New York, 1998 (a largely academic exploration of this issue).
5 **Robert Coles,** 'Robert Coles, the crayon man of Harvard, talks about our "children of crisis"', *People Weekly*, vol. 5, no. 2, January 1976.
6 **Po Bronson** & Ashley Merryman, *NurtureShock: New Thinking about Children*, Twelve, New York, 2009, especially chapter 1. Reviewed by Pulitzer-Prize winning columnist George F. Will, 'Self-esteem, self-destruction', *Washington Post*, 4 March 2010.

7 **From a report** entitled 'The Ethics of American Youth: 2002', The Josephson Institute, Center for Youth Ethics, Los Angeles, http://charactercounts.org/programs/reportcard/2002/index.html.
8 **Summarised** from John Irvine, 'Praising Children', 2007.
9 **Baumeister,** *Psychological Science in the Public Interest.*
10 **From the American Psychiatric Association's,** *Diagnostic and Statistical Manual of Mental Disorders: DSM-5*, 5th edn, American Psychiatric Association, Arlington, 2013, pp. 669–72.
11 **Twenge,** *The Narcissism Epidemic*; Jean M. Twenge & Joshua D. Foster, 'Birth cohort increases in narcissistic personality traits among American college students, 1982–2009', *Social Psychological and Personality Science*, vol 1, no. 1, January 2010, pp. 99–106; episode entitled 'Narcissism', *Insight*, SBS TV, 12 April 2011, http://www.sbs.com.au/insight/episode/watchonline/366/Narcissism.
12 **See, for example,** Twenge, *The Narcissism Epidemic*, 2009; Baumeister, *Psychological Science in the Public Interest*, 2003; Lillian G. Katz, 'Distinctions between narcissism and self-esteem: implications for practice', *Perspectives from ERIC/EECE: A Monograph Series*, no. 5, October 1993, http://www.eric.ed.gov/PDFS/ED363452.pdf.
13 **Jeanna Bryner,** 'Big generation gaps in work attitudes revealed', *LiveScience*, 10 March 2010, http://www.livescience.com/6195-big-generation-gaps-work-attitudes-revealed.html, reporting Jean M. Twenge et al., 'Generational differences in work values: leisure and extrinsic values increasing, social and intrinsic values decreasing', *Journal of Management*, vol. 36, no. 5, September 2010, pp. 1117–42.
14 **Laura L. Smith** & Charles Elliott, *Hollow Kids: Recapturing the Soul of a Generation Lost to the Self-Esteem Myth*, Forum, Roseville CA, 2001; also Dan Kindlon, *Too Much of a Good Thing: Raising Children of Character in an Indulgent Age*, Miramax/Hyperion, New York, 2003.
15 **Shari Kirchner,** 'Not special after all, just useless', Heckler, *SMH*, 5 October 2009. Used by permission. This work has been licensed by Copyright Agency Limited (CAL). Except as permitted by the Copyright Act, you must not re-use this work without the permission of

the copyright owner or CAL.
16 **Nina H. Shokraii**, 'The self-esteem fraud: feel-good education does not lead to academic success', *USA Today Magazine*, vol. 126, no. 2632, January 1998; similarly, Salerno, *SHAM*, chapter 10.
17 **Anna Patty**, 'Helicopter parents not doing enough to let children fail', *SMH*, 3 April 2010, and 'Reality check: abandon false praise, principals say', *SMH*, 7 April 2010. Both articles provoked numerous comments and letters from readers, the majority supportive.
18 **See posts entitled** 'Self-Esteem' (Parts 1 and 2), 5 and 12 April 2009, http://teachingbattleground.wordpress.com/2009/04/05/self-esteem-part-1.
19 **See, for example,** Richard Colvin, 'Losing faith in self-esteem', *The School Administrator*, February 2000, http://www.aasa.org/SchoolAdministratorArticle.aspx?id=14470?.
20 **Tom Scott**, 'What's the difference between self-esteem and self-respect?', http://www.catholica.com.au/sunday/007_sunday_171206.php, responding to Mackay, *SMH*, 2006.
21 **See, for example,** *Collins English Dictionary*, 2014, http://www.collinsdictionary.com/dictionary/english/self-esteem?; *Merriam-Webster Dictionary*, 2014, http://www.merriam-webster.com/dictionary/self-esteem; *Dictionary.com Unabridged*. Random House, Inc., 2014, http://dictionary.reference.com/browse/self-esteem?s=t.
22 **William G. Huitt**, 'Self and Self-Views', *Educational Psychology Interactive*, Valdosta State University, Valdosta, 2011, http://www.edpsycinteractive.org/topics/self/self.html.
23 **This definition** of self-esteem appears in Nathaniel Branden, *The Psychology of Self-Esteem: A Revolutionary Approach to Self-Understanding that Launched a New Era in Modern Psychology*, Jossey-Bass, San Francisco, 2001, p. 252. A similar definition has been adopted by the National Association for Self-Esteem in the USA. In addition, they advocate personal responsibility and accountability.
24 **Emler, '**Self-esteem', 2001; Baumeister, *Psychological Science in the Public Interest*, 2003.

25 **Robert Campbell** & Walter Foddis, 'Is high self-esteem bad for you?', http://www.atlassociety.org/high-self-esteem-bad-you.
26 **Mackay,** *SMH*, 2006. Used by permission.
27 **Marcia Homiak,** 'Moral Character', in Edward N. Zalta (ed.), *The Stanford Encyclopedia of Philosophy*, Spring 2011 edn, http://plato.stanford.edu/archives/spr2011/entries/moral-character.
28 **William James,** *The Principles of Psychology*, 1890. There are limitations to this simplistic definition, of course. For example, a person who achieves a high level of success by setting the goalposts very low is unlikely to have healthy self-esteem. Nevertheless, James's insightful proposal has proved useful.
29 **Seligman,** *The Optimistic Child*, p. 36.
30 **Note that the term** 'doing well' has many shades of meanings in common usage. My usage of the term 'doing well' always encompasses engaging positively with others and behaving well towards them. Whenever our positive engagement with the world is *primarily* aimed at achieving benefits for others, our doing well also becomes doing good.
31 **Seligman,** *The Optimistic Child*, p. 36.
32 **Seligman,** 'Forum on Depression'.
33 **For more information** visit The Positive Psychology Center, http://www.ppc.sas.upenn.edu/index.html.
34 **Martin E. P. Seligman** & Mihaly Csikszentmihaly, 'Positive psychology: an introduction', *American Psychologist*, vol. 55, no. 1, Jan. 2000, pp. 5–14, http://www.ppc.sas.upenn.edu/ppintroarticle.pdf.
35 **Seligman,** 'Forum on Depression'.
36 **Seligman,** *Learned Optimism*.
37 **Ibid.;** Seligman, 'Forum on Depression';
38 **Seligman,** 'Forum on Depression'.
39 **Ehrenreich,** *Smile or Die*, p. 199. Seligman has pointed out that the 'positive psychology movement' he founded bears no resemblance to the 'positive thinking movement', which he says is unproven and dangerous. He cautions against confusing the two approaches (Seligman, *Flourish*, pp. 201–202; Martin E. P. Seligman, *Authentic Happiness: Using*

the *New Positive Psychology to Realise Your Potential for Lasting Fulfilment*, Random House Australia, Sydney, 2002, pp. 96, 288–9). Unfortunately, Ehrenreich does not seem to have made this distinction and includes Seligman's approach in her condemnation.
40 **See** http://www.ppc.sas.upenn.edu/prpsum.htm, http://www.apa.org/research/action/school.aspx; Seligman, *Flourish*, chapter 5.
41 **Seligman,** *The 7.30 Report*, 2009; Seligman, *Flourish*, pp. 85–93.
42 **See** http://www.education.gov.uk/schools/teachingandlearning/curriculum/secondary/b00198880/pshee/ks3/personal, 25 November 2011.
43 **Lauren Slater,** 'The trouble with self-esteem'.

Chapter 9. How Have We Become So Self-Oriented?

1 **Adam Smith,** *An Inquiry into the Nature and Causes of the Wealth of Nations*, 1776; quotation is from *The Theory of Moral Sentiments*, 1759, http://www.adamsmith.org/quotes. Smith, who was Professor of Moral Philosophy at Glasgow University, is now known as the father of the theory of capitalism.
2 **Slater,** 'The trouble with self-esteem'.
3 **Etzioni,** *The Spirit of Community*, p. 8.
4 **Abraham H. Maslow,** 'A theory of human motivation', *Psychological Review*, vol. 50, no. 4, July 1943, pp. 370–96, http://psychclassics.yorku.ca/Maslow/motivation.htm, and his book *Motivation and Personality*, Harper, New York, 1954.
5 **Theodore Roszak,** *The Making of a Counter Culture: Reflections on the Technocratic Society and Its Youthful Opposition*, University of California, Berkeley, 1995, p. xxxiv.
6 **For a detailed analysis** of the flow of change in Western culture towards an intense inward journey and a new religious consciousness during that era, see Eugene Taylor, *Shadow Culture: Psychology and Spirituality in America*, Counterpoint, Washington, 1999. Mainstream culture was also affected. In 1966, the cover of *Time* magazine was asking 'Is God dead?', the perception being that perhaps he was; by 1971, the

cover featured 'The Jesus Revolution'.
7 **Steven M. Tipton,** *Getting Saved from the Sixties: The Transformation of Moral Meaning in American Culture,* University of California Press, Berkeley, 1982; Arthur Marwick *The Sixties: Cultural Revolution in Britain, France, Italy and the United States, c. 1958–c. 1974,* Oxford University Press, Oxford, 1998.
8 **Doug McAdam,** *Freedom Summer,* Oxford University Press, New York, 1988.
9 **Norman Vincent Peale,** *The Power of Positive Thinking,* 1952; *Positive Imaging: The Powerful Way to Change Your Life,* 1952; *You Can If You Think You Can,* 1974; all published by Prentice-Hall, New York. The 'power of positive thinking' attitude criticised in this section is quite different from the notion of 'positive psychology' as introduced by Martin Seligman (described in chapter 8). Some commentators have failed to grasp this distinction.
10 **See chapter 7,** in 'Religious Gurus'.
11 **In 1976** French sociologist Jacques Ellul commented that an anomaly of the twentieth century was the fanatical search for freedom and the development of numerous global and local freedom movements despite the almost universal belief in determinism (Jacques Ellul, *The Ethics of Freedom,* G. W. Bromiley (trans.), Eerdmans, Grand Rapids, 1976).
12 **Although Branden** has expressed his concern as a psychologist about certain aspects of Rand's teachings, he still champions the core of her philosophy on his website; see http://nathanielbranden.com/the-benefits-and-hazards-of-the-philosophy-of-ayn-rand-mp3, http://nathanielbranden.com/discussions.
13 **Branden,** *The Psychology of Self-Esteem,* 2001. In the preface and epilogue of this anniversary edition Branden attempts to correct misconceptions about his teachings on self-esteem that arose after release of the first edition in 1969.
14 **Attributed to** Nathaniel Branden in an online description of his book *Honoring the Self: The Psychology of Confidence and Respect,* Bantam, New York, 1985, http://www.amazon.com/

Honoring-Self-Self-Esteem-Personal-Tranformation/dp/0553268147.
15 **Carol Craig,** 'Impracticality of the concept,' 2006, http://www.centreforconfidence.co.uk/pp/overview.php?p=c2lkPTY=. Another factor may have been the long gap between the publication of Branden's *The Psychology of Self-Esteem* in 1969 and the embellishments and provisos he added in *The Six Pillars of Self-Esteem*, which was not released until 1994, almost 25 years after the self-esteem movement had already taken off.
16 **Branden now places** a strong emphasis on the doing well aspect of self-esteem and has addressed common misconceptions, http://www.nathanielbranden.com/discussions/self-esteem/answering-misconceptions-about-self-esteem.
17 **Kelsey Munro,** 'Youth skim surface of life with constant use of social media', *SMH*, 20 April 2013, http://www.smh.com.au/digital-life/digital-life-news/youth-skim-surface-of-life-with-constant-use-of-social-media-20130419-2i5lr.html.
18 **Psychological anthropologist** and historian Anthony Wallace recognised a trend towards new personalised, fragmented ways of forming worldviews and coined the term 'mazeways' to describe this phenomenon in *Religion: An Anthropological View*, Random House, New York, 1966.
19 **Mitchell Grady,** a university student, on *Q&A*, ABC TV, 31 May 2010. For a deeper analysis of this issue, see Turkle, *Alone Together*.
20 **Nicholas Carr,** 'How the internet makes us stupid', *Daily Telegraph* (UK), 27 August 2010; Nicholas Carr, *The Shallows: How the Internet Is Changing the Way We Think, Read and Remember*, W. W. Norton & Co, New York, 2010; and see chapter 4, endnotes 35 and 36.
21 **Susan Greenfield,** 'How digital culture is rewiring our brains', *SMH*, 7 August 2012.
22 **Rachel Browne,** 'Screen violence changing young brains: researchers', *SMH*, 5 October 2013. In response to a recent spate of unprovoked and sometimes fatal one-punch assaults on young men in Sydney streets, a 19-year-old Sydney Swans footballer has highlighted the desensitising effects of excessive exposure to escalating violence in games, movies, TV and social media, especially among the many young people who are no

longer provided with a foundation of ethical principles and moral acuity by parents and schools; see Brandon Jack, 'King-hit assaults show moral sense skewed by intoxicatingly violent culture', *SMH*, 7 January 2014.

23 **Rushkoff,** *Present Shock*, chapter 2.

24 **Response of Gervase Markham** in Janna Quitney Anderson & Lee Rainie, 'The future of social relations', Pew Research Center Report, 2 July 2010, p. 11, http://www.pewinternet.org/2010/07/02/the-future-of-social-relations-2. Some would argue that this is already happening.

25 **John F. Helliwell** & Haifang Huang, 'Comparing the happiness effects of real and on-line friends', Working Paper (National Bureau of Economic Research), January 2013, http://www.nber.org/papers/w18690.

26 **Turkle,** *Alone Together*, pp. 280–281.

27 **Mitch Albom,** *Tuesdays with Morrie: An Old Man, a Young Man and Life's Greatest Lesson*, 10th anniversary edn, Broadway, New York, 2007 (a series of discussions between a student and his Jewish professor who is dying). A movie based on this book was released in 1999.

28 *Macquarie Dictionary Online,* 2014.

Chapter 10: The Impact of Self-Esteem Myths on Society

1 **Jimmy Carter's** televised speech entitled 'Crisis of Confidence', 15 July 1979, http://millercenter.org/president/speeches/detail/3402.

2 **See text excerpts** from the movie *The 11th Hour,* 2007, http://www.digitalnpq.org/archive/2007_fall/12_dicaprio_etal.html.

3 **Robert H. Frank,** 'Income inequality: too big to ignore', *The New York Times,* 16 October 2010. He reported that 'the share of total income going to the top 1 percent of earners, which stood at 8.9 percent in 1976, rose to 23.5 percent by 2007, but during the same period, the average inflation-adjusted hourly wage declined by more than 7 percent.' In this context, I see the huge increases in income paid to top

executives compared with wage increases for those providing essential services and the battlers as self-indulgent obscenity. See also Barbara Ehrenreich, *Nickel and Dimed: On (Not) Getting by in America*, Metropolitan Books, New York, 2001.
4 **Caroline West,** *SMH*.
5 **See David Humphries,** 'Season of our disconnect', *SMH*, 2 July 2011. He writes about the ways in which 'the switch in society's focus from "we" to "me" has given free rein to superficial and populist politics'.
6 **Henry Samuel,** 'Rich offer to pay more tax to ease EU debt', *SMH*, 26 November 2012. Buffet would like to see the rich in the USA paying a minimum tax of 30% on incomes of $1 million to $10 million and 35% above that; see http://www.reuters.com/article/2012/11/26/us-buffett-tax-idUSBRE8AP0LY20121126.
7 **Hamilton,** *The Freedom Paradox*, p. 19.
8 **Richard Eckersley,** 'Why values matter: the individual and community', Communities in Control Conference, Melbourne, June 2004, http://www.ourcommunity.com.au/files/eckersleyppt.pdf; see also Eckersley, *Well & Good*, p. 255.
9 **Jeremy Rifkin,** *The Age of Access: The New Culture of Hypercapitalism, Where All of Life is a Paid-for Experience*, J. P. Tarcher/Putnam, New York, 2001, chapter 9. Rifkin is founder and President of The Foundation on Economic Trends.
10 **From** 'United Nations Human Development Report 1998', chapter 1, p. 37; this paragraph is based on Anup Shah's summary, http://www.globalissues.org/article/26/poverty-facts-and-stats.
11 **See** http://www.un.org/millennium/declaration/ares552e.pdf.
12 **Outcome document** of the Millenium Development Goals Summit 2010 and The Monterey Consensus of 2002.
13 **International Development Strategy** for the Second United Nations Development Decade, UN General Assembly Resolution 2626 (XXV), October 24, 1970, paragraph 43.
14 **In 2012,** the UK contributed 0.56%, Australia 0.32% and the USA 0.19% (ranked 5th, 13th and 18th of 24 countries, respectively), http://

www.oecd.org/dac/stats/oda2012-interactive.htm. Major donors' aid fell by nearly 3% between 2010 and 2011, breaking a long trend of annual increases, http://www.oecd.org/dac/stats/developmentaidtodevelopingcountriesfallsbecauseofglobalrecession.htm.

15 **Anup Shah,** http://www.globalissues.org/article/35/foreign-aid-development-assistance; Jeremy D. Sachs, *The End of Poverty: How We Can Make It Happen in Our Lifetime*, Penguin, London, 2005.

16 **Pekka Hirvonen,** Global Policy Forum, 2005, http://www.globalpolicy.org/component/content/article/240/45056.html. A UN official's report in 2008 stating that as many as 300,000 people may have died due to the then five-year-old conflict in Darfur in the Sudan received only a 10-second evening news spot. On the other hand, the 2004 Boxing Day tsunami near Indonesia, which also resulted in a horrific loss of live (an estimated 230,000 deaths), received concentrated, ongoing coverage in the Australian press and raised vast amounts of public money for relief. Was this imbalance due, at least in part, to the importance of good relations between Australia and its near neighbour Indonesia?

17 **Sachs,** *The End of Poverty.*

18 **See documentary** *U2: Rock Crusade*, 2000, http://www.theage.com.au/tv/show/u2-rock-crusade/u2-rock-crusade-20111028-1mnl3.html.

19 **See** http://givingpledge.org, a welcome initiative of Bill Gates and Warren Buffet. Unfortunately, the rhetoric and generous promises of nations (and individual benefactors) is not always matched by actual performance. For example, $5.3 billion in aid was promised at a conference two months after Haiti's January 2010 earthquake but four months later less than 2% had been handed over; see http://articles.cnn.com/2010-07-15/world/haiti.donations_1_haitian-government-pledges-aid.

20 **For inspiration** you could read Sachs, *The End of Poverty*, 2005; E. Fritz Schumacher, *Small Is Beautiful: Economics As If People Mattered*, Hartley & Marks, Point Roberts, 1999; Ronald A. Sider, *Rich Christians in an Age of Hunger: Moving from Affluence to Generosity*, Thomas Nelson, Nashville, 2005; Peter Singer, *The Life You Can Save: Acting Now to End World Poverty*, Random House, New York, 2009.

21 **Fido is an Australian online** skills-matching service that connects skilled, experienced volunteers with not-for-profit organisations for short- or long-term, local or overseas positions, http://www.fido.com.au. See also http://www.worldvision.com.au/act/Volunteer.aspx, http://www.volunteeringaustralia.org. Goals and strategies of organisations and the proportion of donated funds that reach the disadvantaged can be checked online, e.g. http://www.choice.com.au/reviews-and-tests/money/investing/advice/charities.aspx. See also http://www.philanthropy.org.au/images/site/misc/Tools__Resources/Publications/PA_A-Guide-to-Giving.pdf.
22 **Barbara Ehrenreich,** *Smile or Die.*
23 **Martin Seligman,** 'Forum on Depression'.
24 **Branden,** *The Psychology of Self-Esteem*, p. 253 and back cover.

Chapter 11. Finding Identity and Meaning

1 **See** http://en.musicplayon.com/play?v=238579.
2 **John Smith,** *Advance Australia Where? A Lack of Meaning in a Land of Plenty*, Anzea, Sydney, 1988. Australian Christian Book of the Year Award, 1989.
3 **Rick Warren,** *The Purpose Driven Life: What on Earth Am I Here For?*, Zondervan, Grand Rapids, 2002. Note that I do not endorse all the teachings and arguments of this author.
4 **Hamilton,** *Affluenza*, p. 183.
5 **Marcia Homiak,** 'Moral Character', in *The Stanford Encyclopedia of Philosophy*, Spring 2011 edn, Edward N. Zalta (ed.), http://plato.stanford.edu/archives/spr2011/entries/moral-character.
6 **Abridged from** http://www.thehappinessinstitute.com/freeproducts/docs/CHOOSE%20handout%20summary.pdf. This approach also tends to give the impression that happiness is entirely dependent on choices we can control, ignoring the many factors in our lives over which we have no control. For me, this smacks of the be-whatever-you-want-to-be myth.

7 **Viktor E. Frankl,** *The Unheard Cry for Meaning: Psychotherapy and Humanism*, Touchstone, New York, 1979, p. 36; and televised presentation 'Interview, South Africa, 1985 (Part II)', http://logotherapy.univie.ac.at/e/clipgallery.html.
8 **Mackay,** *SMH*, 2010. Mackay develops these ideas in his book *The Good Life*, 2013. While I agree with Mackay's comments about many issues, I do not share his ambivalence or possible negativity towards the spiritual dimension of life. Nor do I believe that living by the Golden Rule (treating others as you would like to be treated yourself), as he advocates, is in itself sufficient to ensure a maximally meaningful and satisfying life. However, I agree strongly with him that concern for others is a very important aspect of a life well lived.
9 **Seligman,** *Authentic Happiness*, pp. 137–61, 249; VIA Test of Character Strengths, http://www.authentichappiness.sas.upenn.edu; Seligman, *Flourish*, p. 121.
10 **See, for example,** Kathleen Doheny, 'Acts of kindness can make you happier', 24 January 2013, http://health.usnews.com/health-news/news/articles/2013/01/24/acts-of-kindness-can-make-you-happier.
11 **Eckersley,** *Well & Good*, p. 86.
12 **Hamilton,** *Affluenza*, p. 182.
13 **Hamilton,** *The Freedom Paradox*, pp. 6, 18; quotation, p. 6.
14 **Hamilton,** *Affluenza*, p. 183.
15 **Headey,** *Proceedings of the National Academy of Sciences*.
16 **Lara B. Aknin et al.,** 'Prosocial spending and well-being: cross-cultural evidence for a psychological universal', National Bureau of Economic Research, Working Paper No. 16415, Cambridge [USA], September 2010; an analysis of data from 136 countries. See also Lynn E. Alden & Jennifer E. Trew, 'If it makes you happy: engaging in kind acts increases positive affect in socially anxious individuals', *Emotion*, vol. 13, no. 1, February 2013, pp. 64–75.
17 **See** http://fcsministries.org.
18 **See** http://www.homelesstaskforce.org/aboutus.html.
19 **This is still operating,** http://satlmarketplace.org.

20 **Mark E. Koltko-Rivera,** 'Rediscovering the later version of Maslow's hierarchy of needs: self-transcendence and opportunities for theory, research, and unification', *Review of General Psychology*, vol. 10, no. 4, Dec. 2006, pp. 302–317; Abraham H. Maslow, *The Farther Reaches of Human Nature*, The Viking Press, New York, 1971. For a brief summary of Maslow's amended theory, see W. Huitt, 'Maslow's hierarchy of needs', *Educational Psychology Interactive*, Valdosta State University, Valdosta, 2007, http://www.edpsycinteractive.org/topics/conation/maslow.html.

21 **Frankl,** *Man's Search for Meaning*; and 'Interview, South Africa, 1985 (Part II)'.

22 **Frankl believed** that people thrive on and desire the tension of striving for some worthy goal. He even suggests that pursuing extreme sports, such as skiing, abseiling or motor racing, may be an intuitive reaction to our comfortable Western world, in which we otherwise do our best to avoid discomfort and challenge; Frankl, *The Unheard Cry for Meaning*.

23 **Frankl,** *The Unheard Cry for Meaning*, pp. 20–21.

24 **Maslow himself** recognised exceptions to his theory of the hierarchical nature of needs, as indicated in his later scholarly works; see Maslow, *The Farther Reaches of Human Nature*, 1971. Also at odds with Maslow's original theory is the fact that members of cultures living in bare physical survival mode, at the level of the most basic human need, will nevertheless lay aside a little of whatever they have to offer to their gods or to maintain social or tribal order. This is illustrated by the story of my visit to El Salvador (chapter 4).

25 **Victor Frankl,** TV interview, 'Religion and ultimate meaning, 1990', http://logotherapy.univie.ac.at/e/clipgallery.html.

26 *Macquarie Dictionary Online, 2014*.

27 **From Fragments,** quoted in Erich Fromm, *Man for Himself: An Inquiry into the Psychology of Ethics*, Open Road Integrated Media, New York, 2013, p. 38.

28 **Kinlaw,** *Let's Start with Jesus*, p. 76.

29 **Ibid.**

30 **Frankl,** *The Unheard Cry for Meaning.*

Chapter 12. Exploring the Spiritual Dimension

1 **Isaiah 55:2,** *The Holy Bible*; also recorded in Jewish Scriptures.
2 **Morris Berman,** *The Reenchantment of the World*, Bantam, Toronto, 1984. He believes that modern man and woman are less autonomous and more desperate for salvation than their counterparts were at any other time in history.
3 **Matthew Arnold,** *The Poems of Matthew Arnold 1849–1864*, Elibron Classics, Adamanta Media Corporation, Boston, 2005; first published 1906.
4 **Manning Clark,** *A History of Australia*, vol. 4, Melbourne University Press, Melbourne, 1979.
5 **Ibid.,** p. 231.
6 **If the proposition** of Divine purpose is valid, the value of the individual would be affirmed both extrinsically and intrinsically. We would have value conferred by God and we would have intrinsic value because of the nature of being created.
7 **Viktor E. Frankl,** *The Unconscious God: Psychotherapy and Theology*, Simon & Schuster, New York, 1975, pp. 61–2.
8 **Psalms 19:1–4 and 8:3–4,** *The Holy Bible*; David's psalms are also recorded in Jewish Scriptures.
9 **Phillip Adams,** 'Don't worry, be melancholy', *The Australian*, 17–18 April 2010.
10 **Sheridan Voysey,** *Unseen Footprints: Encountering the Divine along the Journey of Life*, Hudson Lion, Oxford, 2007.
11 **Adam Lindsay Gordon,** *The Poetical Works of Adam Lindsay Gordon*, Adamant Media, Boston, 2006, p. xix. First published in 1913 by Ward & Co, London.
12 **Fritjof Capra,** *The Tao of Physics: An Exploration of the Parallels between Modern Physics and Eastern Mysticism*, 25th anniversary edn, Shambhal, Boston, 2000.
13 **Charles Birch,** *On Purpose*, New South Wales University Press, Sydney,

1990, p. xv.
14 **Taylor,** *Shadow Culture*, 1999. He believes this emerging shadow culture, as he terms it, triumphed over traditional opinion, promoting a revolution in concepts within the fields of both psychology and religion. Others have shown that the hotbeds of alternative spiritualities were the regions of the USA in which adherence to formal religion had declined; see Roger Finke & Rodney Stark, *Churching of America, 1776–1990: Winners and Losers in our Religious Economy*, Rutgers University, New Brunswick, 1992.

Chapter 13. The Most Seductive Myth of All

1 **Taylor,** *Shadow Culture*, 1999.
2 **Ross Douthat,** 'Heaven and Nature', *The New York Times*, 20 December 2009.
3 **Loomans,** *The Lovables in the Kingdom of Self-Esteem*, 1991.
4 **See** http://www.brainyquote.com/quotes/authors/o/oprah_winfrey.html.
5 **Ibid.**
6 **Wayne W. Dyer,** *Your Sacred Self: Making the Decision to Be Free*, HarperCollins, New York, 1995, pp. 2, 316.
7 **See** http://www.askjudymoss.com.au/WHAT_IS_GUIDANCE.
8 **From** http://www.newworldencyclopedia.org/entry/Ralph_Waldo_Emerson. In contrast, Frankl speaks of an inner 'unconscious God', who is both transcendent and profoundly personal and whose presence needs to be acknowledged to bring us to 'suprameaning'; see George C. Boeree, 'Viktor Frankl. 1905–1997', 2006, http://webspace.ship.edu/cgboer/frankl.html.
9 **This trend** is even more evident today than when first noted by Friedrich von Hayek in 1944; see Hamilton, *The Freedom Paradox*, 2011, p. 8.
10 **See** http://www.poets.org/poetsorg/poem/invictus.
11 **A saying often attributed** to the great English intellectual G. K. Chesterton.

12 **In the rush** to such alternatives, most seem to have forgotten that it was the substantial failure of such belief systems that contributed greatly to the rapid spread of fledgling Christianity from the centre to the margins of the Roman Empire; Rodney Stark, *The Rise of Christianity: How the Obscure, Marginal, Jesus Movement Became the Dominant Religious Force in the Western World in a Few Centuries*, HarperCollins, San Francisco, 1997.

13 **Sadly,** many of these traditions have been 'strip-mined' for the pampered minority of the world's population. There are now exotic substitutes for old spiritualities that demand less personal sacrifice and bypass the old religious concepts of sin and guilt for wrongdoing.

14 **Headey,** Proceedings of the National Academy of Sciences, 2010; participants were mainly Christian with a Muslim minority.

15 **Bruce Headey et al.,** 'Authentic happiness theory supported by impact of religion on life satisfaction: A longitudinal analysis with data for Germany', *Journal of Positive Psychology*, vol. 5, no. 1, January 2010, pp. 73–82.

16 **Dick Gross,** 'On Christmas and suffering', SMH, 24 December 2010.

17 **Hamilton,** *Affluenza*, p. 183.

18 **The story of Jesus** is told by four of his contemporaries in *The Holy Bible* in the Gospels of Matthew, Mark, Luke and John. Luke is written in narrative form. Various translations of the Bible, including modern English versions, can be found at http://www.biblegateway.com.

19 **Books you may find helpful** include: John Dickson, *If I Were God I'd Make Myself Clearer: Searching for Clarity in A World Full of Claims*, 2003 and *Simply Christianity: Beyond Religion*, 1999, both published by Matthias Media, Sydney; Lee Strobel, *The Case for Christ: A Journalists's Personal Investigation of the Evidence for Jesus*, Zondervan, Grand Rapids, 1998. To delve more deeply, see John R. W. Stott, *Basic Christianity*, InterVarsity Press, Downers Grove, 2006; John Dickson, *A Spectator's Guide to Jesus: An Introduction to the Man from Nazareth*, Lion UK, Oxford, 2008. Also, many people have spoken to me of the life-changing consequences of attending the much celebrated Alpha Course, which is offered by churches in many countries throughout the world and supported by all the main Christian

denominations, see http://alpha.org.au, http://www.alpha.org.

20 **Leesha McKenny,** 'Atheists call on like-minded to declare lack of religion in census', *SMH,* 5 February 2011. Campaign director Malcolm Williams commented: 'Some Christians were quite indignant [about the poster], while lots of people who aren't churchgoers were knocking on church doors saying "thank you"', presumably for encouraging them to see Jesus in a new light.

21 **Galatians 5:22–23,** *The Holy Bible.* Of course, one does not need to be a Christian to exhibit the virtues listed, but it is a tragedy when those who claim to be Christians show little evidence of them.

22 **For more about** the extraordinary expansion of this charismatic faith, which was largely rejected by the Jewish society in which it was birthed, see Rodney Stark, *The Rise of Christianity,* 1997.

Chapter 14. Self-Esteem and Self-Surrender: The Ultimate Paradox

1 **See** http://www.piercedhearts.org/purity_heart_morality/mother_teresa_address_united_nations.htm.

2 **Because gender** is a distinctly human characteristic, I see it as a non-issue when describing a transcendent higher power. Unfortunately, there are no pronouns in the English language that allow us to express this idea. I have opted for the widely accepted convention of using the masculine singular. See http://en.wikipedia.org/wiki/Gender_of_the_Holy_Spirit; Clark H. Pinnock, *The Flame of Love: A Theology of the Holy Spirit,* InterVarsity Press, Downers Grove, 1996.

3 **Luke 17:33,** *The Holy Bible.*

4 **By George Matheson** (1842–1906), a brilliant student of philosophy and divinity at Glasgow University who became virtually blind by the age of eighteen; published 1890.

5 **R. S. Pine-Coffin** (trans.), *St Augustine's Confessions,* Penguin, London, 1961, p. 21.

6 **Robert J. Hillman** with Coral Chamberlain & Linda Harding, *Healing*

and Wholeness: Reflections on the Healing Ministry, Regnum, Oxford, 2003, p. 114. He alludes to Romans 12:3 in *The Holy Bible:* 'Do not think of yourself more highly than you ought, but rather think of yourself with sober judgment'.

7 **Philippians 2:6–8** in Eugene H. Peterson, *The Message: The Bible in Contemporary Language,* NavPress, Colorado Springs, 2002. Many of my non-religious friends were strangely touched by the secular song of the 1990s, 'What if God was one of us'. According to this quotation, he was!

8 **This story is recorded** in the Jewish Torah, the Christian Bible and the Muslim Koran.

9 **Yahweh is the English transliteration** of the Jewish sacred name of God, as used in the Bible.

10 **In recordings** of pastor Martin Luther King Jr's famous 'I've been to the mountaintop' speech, the listener senses in the timbre of his voice and the compelling nature of his rhetoric that he spoke not simply on his own behalf but with the ultimate higher authority, before which even the mighty American Supreme Court must tremble, http://www.americanrhetoric.com/speeches/mlkivebeentothemountaintop.htm. I believe it is this sense of Divine authority that is also the backdrop to the incredibly powerful identity of the Jewish people that has enabled them to survive enormous hardships and persecution.

Other books by John Smith

On the Side of the Angels

Advance Australia Where?

Cutting Edge

This is John Smith

Searching for Satisfaction: Rock's Search for Faith and Meaning

Sharpening the Cutting Edge

The Origins, Nature, and Significance of the Jesus Movement as a Revitalization Movement